THE FAST TRACK TO PROFIT

An Insider's Guide to Exploiting the World's Best Internet Technologies

Lee G. Caldwell

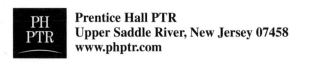

Prentice Hall PTR
Upper Saddle River, New Jersey 07458
www.phptr.com

Library of Congress Cataloging-in-Publication Data

Caldwell, Lee.
    Fast track to profit : an insider's guide to exploiting the world's
best Internet technologies / Lee Caldwell.
    p. cm. -- (Hewlett-Packard professional books)
Includes index.
    ISBN 0-13-046347-7
    1. Electronic commerce. 2. Information technology--Management. I.
Title. II. Series.
    HF5548.32 .C34 2002
    658'.054678--dc21

                                                        2002006971

Editorial/Production Supervision: *Nicholas Radhuber*
Acquisitions Editor: *Jill Harry*
Editorial Assistant: *Jeanie Joe*
Marketing Manager: *Dan DePasquale*
Manufacturing Buyer: *Maura Zaldivar*
Cover Design: *Anthony Gemmellaro*
Cover Design Director: *Jerry Votta*

Manager, Hewlett-Packard Retail Book Publishing: *Patricia Pekary*

PH
PTR
© 2003 by Hewlett-Packard Company
Published by Pearson Education, Inc.
Publishing as Prentice Hall PTR
Upper Saddle River, NJ 07458

Prentice Hall books are widely used by corporations and government agencies
for training, marketing, and resale.

The publisher offers discounts on this book when ordered in bulk quantities.
For more information, contact Corporate Sales Department, phone: 800-382-3419;
fax: 201-236-7141; email: corpsales@prenhall.com. Or write: Corporate Sales
Department, Prentice Hall PTR, One Lake Street, Upper Saddle River, NJ 07458.

Product and company names mentioned herein are the trademarks or registered
trademarks of their respective owners.

Printed in the United States of America

10 9 8 7 6 5 4 3 2 1

ISBN 0-13-046347-7

Pearson Education LTD.
Pearson Education Australia PTY, Limited
Pearson Education Singapore, Pte. Ltd
Pearson Education North Asia Ltd
Pearson Education Canada, Ltd.
Pearson Educación de Mexico, S.A. de C.V.
Pearson Education—Japan
Pearson Education Malaysia, Pte. Ltd

Contents

Foreword

Just What the Doctor Ordered

Having just read Lee Caldwell's manuscript for his book, *The Fast Track to Profit: An Insider's Guide to Exploiting the World's Best Internet Technologies,* I am pleased to let you know that Dr. Caldwell's prescription for business success will undoubtedly save you and your future customers time, money and a whole lot of headaches.

Every business has the challenge of delivering the customer results that will support their business models and business strategies. Even when the business processes supporting these customer results utilizes the best internet technologies, this book will provide the reader with clear prescriptions that will improve the opportunity for success.

I recommend that you use this book to understand the business secrets of successful companies and the business disasters of unsuccessful companies. Lee Caldwell offers a truly unique perspective on both. Lee has experience in strategy development, technology integration, and business alignment and execution. The combination of his experience and a refined ability to observe and evaluate business results make this book particularly pertinent at this time.

I think you'll particularly appreciate the way this book features tremendously helpful insight into some of the world's largest vertical industries. Whether you work in a small company or a Fortune 50 company, you'll learn about some of the most practical, remarkable, and rock-solid secrets that you can apply to your own business practices.

Study the insider secrets you'll find herein, and take full advantage of them. In doing so, I am certain that you will increase your chances for taking the fast track to profit.

Denny Georg
Hewlett-Packard Company

Preface

"If everything seems under control, you're just not going fast enough."

Such are the prophetic words of winning racecar driver Mario Andretti. If it has been too long since you felt the thrill—the pure exhilaration—of victory, and you're hungry to take the checkered flag, there's a very good chance that you've come to the right place. But, be warned...

This is not a book for the shy and timid. Similarly, this is not a book for the reckless and out-of-control. Rather, *The Fast Track to Profit* is a book for people who want to accelerate their paths to profit, with a new breed of speed and precision and agility.

You have a choice. You can endure the frustration of unacceptable profit levels, or you can follow my "Step-by-Step Owner's Manual" and find that in no time flat, you can get your company on the fast track to profit.

Comedian Steven Wright recently pondered, "I watched the Indy 500, and I was thinking that if they left earlier they wouldn't have to go so fast." Have you talked and planned and strategized about how to increase your company's profits until you're blue in the face? And for all your efforts, do you see nothing but smashed bugs all over your proverbial corporate windshield? Are you sick of having your motor idling *behind* the starting line, while you end up eating your competition's dust? Are you ready for tangible, impressive, bottom-line results that will markedly improve your profits in record time?

If so, read on! Fasten your seat belt and grab the wheel with all your might! Prepare for the ride of your life!

Ladies and gentlemen…it's time to start your engines…

Acknowledgments

"**I** not only use all the brains that I have, but all that I can borrow." Such were the words of wisdom from President Woodrow Wilson. Great approach, Mr. President. In fact, I like it so much that I've used it with great pleasure as I've worked on *The Fast Track to Profit.*

Among the many brains that I've tapped in this book are those of Vinton Cerf and Robert Kahn.

Vinton Cerf has shown remarkable leadership and vision in taking the Internet where no Internet has gone before. He has taught me that we can take the Internet to every corner of the world, take it into every application, and make every process work together. Vint's personal leadership through the Internet Society has helped the industry operate under a codified set of professional ethics. He has such tremendous vision and drive.

Bob Kahn was the director of the Information Processing Techniques Office (IPTO) of the Defense Advanced Research Projects Agency (DARPA) when the whole Internet project started. Bob was the visionary and practical facilitator of every major growth point of the Internet.

Another key source of inspiration for this book came from Larry Landweber, a computer science professor at the University of Wisconsin. Larry was once referred to as the ubiquitous Larry Landweber in a book called

Exploring the Internet. Larry really is the father of international connectivity of the Internet. He established the first international connection to the University College London, which became the first intercontinental link anywhere. Along with Vint, he founded the Internet Society and held a series of international seminars that really helped push Internet technology forward. Larry also helped get the Internet going forward in developing countries.

Two other visionaries from whom I've drawn inspiration are George Sadowski and Stefano Trumpye. Both of these fellows have done tremendous amounts of work in developing countries. Their work, through international seminars and scholarships, has been instrumental in spreading Internet technology throughout the world.

Al Weis, whom I'll talk about later in this book, has done wonders for the practical operation of the Internet, and, to him I tip my hat.

Doug Van Houweling, who used to be the Chief Information Officer (CIO) at the University of Michigan and who now is the president of the University Corporation for Advanced Internet Development (UCIAD), was one of the visionaries, along with Al Weis, who pulled the Internet together from an operations point of view.

Across the pond, in Europe, some amazing leadership has come from Frode Greisen, who managed the European-wide E-Bone and who has led many cross-European networking activities. Kees Neggars, who is with SURFnet in the Netherlands, has done much of the heavy lifting to help the Internet take hold in Europe.

I've also learned a lot from Kilnon Chon, who was with the Korean Education Ministry and who is thought of as the father of advanced networking in Asia.

I'd also like to thank my former manager at International Business Machines (IBM), John Patrick. John single-handedly risked his career inside IBM to make sure the company figured out the Internet at every single stage of its remarkable evolution.

Irving Wladkaski-Berger is the fellow who practically drove the Internet through IBM. He and John were incredible colleagues and terrific sources of inspiration.

At Hewlett-Packard (HP), I'm indebted to Denny Georg, the chief technology officer for our computing organization. He's a real luminary and the leading architect for our internal Information Technology (IT) infrastructure. My manager, Vyomesh Joshi, and my former manager, Carolyn Tichnor, have been enormously supportive.

I also would like to thank Carol Booth, the best, most-connected Internet-oriented assistant. Carol has incredible technical savvy and smarts, the ability to anticipate things, incredible business judgment, and the ability to stay on top of complex technology conversations.

Heartfelt thanks also go to my wonderful wife, Bonnie, and our two children, Alicia and Lee D. I especially appreciate my kids not bugging me too much while I was working on the book.

Finally, I'd like to thank Rosalie Passovoy, a retired principal analyst with the University of California, who edited this book with tremendous skill and care, and Alexander Passovoy, a retired Security Pacific vice president, who generously shared his stories about the banking industry. Rosalie and Alex also contributed something else—or shall I say *someone else*—to this book. They brought my HP colleague and friend, Jan S. Smith, into this world, and, a few decades later, she became the world's greatest writer. I want to thank Jan for her creativity, her boundless energy, her sense of humor, and her amazing way with words.

Using Internet Technologies
to Make Cold, Hard Cash

Taking the fast track to profit by exploiting some of the world's best Internet technologies can yield remarkable results in record time. However, many companies, including yours perhaps, balk at taking this route because of their innate fear of applying new technologies to old and familiar processes.

Resistance to change is nothing new. I suspect that it's been around since the beginning of time. I know it goes back at least as far as the days of my great-grandpa.

I remember my mother telling me about the struggle her grandfather had with his Model T. My great-grandpa was a blacksmith, you see. He knew a lot about horses. Then he got his first car, a Model T. Good ol' great-grandpa was driving into the garage one day and discovered that his Model T didn't respond to his voice commands the way that his horses had. As he drove further into the garage with his new Model T, he yelled out at the top of his lungs, "Whoa!" He ended up taking out the back of the garage when his new car failed to respond.

Just as my great-grandpa struggled at first with the new technology of his day, expect people within your company to agonize through their own upcoming technology adjustment period.

However, contrary to popular belief, making cold, hard cash by applying and exploiting new technologies will always be the easy part of the process-change formula. Staying singularly focused on your customers while reengineering your processes will always be the tough part.

Examples abound of companies that kept their eyes firmly planted on their customers while completely overhauling their basic business models. Consider the wildly successful example of e-Schwab.

1.1 e-Schwab Buys Low and Sells High

An example of a company that sells intangibles, almost exclusively, is e-Schwab. There are no athletic shoes to inventory and distribute or automobiles to move around and showcase. Stocks and mutual funds, for example, are largely computer-generated products. In fact, for the most part, the entire financial services industry sells intangibles made up primarily of IT offerings.

At any point in time, based on the trading that's going on within an individual e-Schwab account, portfolios are electronically updated by a seamless and invisible computer network. However, it's important to note that this was far from the original business model at Schwab.

Today, individual transaction costs are greatly reduced across the board at e-Schwab, freeing up resources for e-Schwab's all-important one-on-one, personalized servicing of each of its customers. How does it do this so effectively?

The folks at e-Schwab took a hard look at the total bucket of resources they could reasonably spend servicing their customers. They decided to invest in the Internet infrastructure needed to make all of their business processes truly world class. The resulting reduction in individual electronic transaction costs freed up all-important resources that they could then spend interacting individually with their customers. This direct service model has paid enormous dividends for e-Schwab. Schwab launched a series of integrated systems in the early 1990s, and, in the third quarter of 1996, it launched e-Schwab.

Online systems captured 43 percent of trades in 1996, with the bulk being through the call-in system. By 2000, the number had jumped to 80 percent of its trades. In the same period, Schwab revenues increased from

$1.4 billion to $5.8 billion, and net profits increased from $172 million to $718 million. That's impressive.

It's an example of how a relatively modest (low) up-front investment in Internet technologies has yielded enormous (high) end-to-end results in a matter of months. This investment also built sustainable competitive advantages and upset the economics of the entire industry.

1.2 Dell Revolutionizes the Process of Big-Ticket

1.2.1 Consumer Purchases

A few years back, you'd be hard-pressed to find someone who honestly believed that consumers would purchase something as expensive as a personal computer through the Internet. However, Dell was ahead of its time, and, as a result, the company has grown into an international technology powerhouse.

It's really a simple concept. Dell made it easy for people to order their personal computers remotely: no driving, no parking lots, no waiting in line, and no lugging the hardware out of the store and into your car.

That's not all that Dell did, though. It created an extraordinarily flexible supply and delivery chain that beats the socks off of all its competitors. Dell is one of the world's best examples of a company that that has been able to reduce its transaction costs by exploiting great Internet technologies. How did Dell do this?

Consider the old model of how personal computers (PCs) were sold in the mid-1980s. At that time, the industry-average manufacturing mark-up was one-third. Then, you had a channel mark-up of one-third, followed by a retail mark-up of still another one-third. In other words, in the 1980s, the average mark-up on PCs was 100 percent.

Today, the average mark-up across the PC industry is about 18 percent. Talk about margins being squeezed!

What Dell has been able to do is capture more of the margin for itself by using its direct-to-the-customer sales model. Amazingly, Dell also has been able to let customers feel like they are having a more personalized experience than they would have had if they went into a crowded Circuit City, for example. At such a store, they would be faced with thousands of

PCs stacked up in aisle after aisle, with seemingly comparable features and prices.

This is a pretty compelling example of how a company can make cold, hard cash fairly quickly by applying Internet technologies to its basic business processes.

By the way, let it be perfectly clear that other companies are studying the Dell model inside and out because it works in such a breakthrough fashion.

By 1997, Dell was producing more than $4 million a day in business through its Internet site. An even larger volume of customers used the site to price and configure systems before ordering over the telephone. By 1999, Dell reported that it maintained more than 40,000 custom Web sites for its corporate and institutional customers.

1.3 Learning from the Mistakes of Others

Who wouldn't want to take the fast track to profit? It seems like most companies would, yet so many have tried and failed. What went wrong?

1.3.1 Mistake #1: Avoiding Traditional Means of Advertising

The most common error that companies make is trying to retrofit an Internet frontend onto their existing systems and processes, while underestimating what it takes to drive people to the Internet in the first place. Companies end up waiting and waiting for business that never comes to their site.

Dell avoided this trap by using a wide range of advertising media and other promotional materials to drive people to its Web site.

It's critically important to remember that you shouldn't do all of your promotion over the Internet. Naturally, some of it can occur there, but much must be done in more conventional ways. This almost symphonic approach to marketing provides the perfect blend to attract customers and to entice them to buy from you through your Web site.

1.3.2 Mistake #2: Failing to be Customer Focused

The second mistake that I've seen occurs when companies design their Internet sites around an organization-centered design, rather than a customer-centered design. What they typically end up with are sites that are very difficult for customers to navigate. Difficulty in navigation leads to difficulty in buying, and it's a deadly combination.

My advice continues to be for companies to invest in the tools that will allow them to study Internet buying patterns, Internet selection patterns, and Internet browsing patterns. By studying these patterns in the early stages of the Internet buying process, companies can relentlessly follow through on what they have learned.

This means that companies must design their Web sites so that they can track where people have gotten lost and where they'd like to go.

Stay customer focused, but keep in mind that you can also make a lot of cold, hard cash by optimizing your internal processes as well.

1.3.3 Mistake #3: Ignoring the Total Customer Experience

Mistakes #1 and #2 can stop business cold before it ever even happens. Mistake #3 can dramatically limit a company's ability to capitalize on customer goodwill and repeat business.

All too often, customers may have a great experience buying from a particular company, but then the company fails to follow through with the total customer experience, meaning every single point at which the customer interacts with a company: before, during, and after the sale. What happens after the order is placed? A great company with a great Web site immediately acknowledges an order, typically through email. Shipping information can be sent, and customers can be kept informed of the status of their orders throughout the process. It's a courtesy customers appreciate and remember.

Consider the Amazon or Dell models. Not only do they immediately send you an email acknowledging and thanking you for your order, they also update you throughout the shipping process and provide a FedEx or United Parcel Service (UPS) tracking system link for each individual order. Customers don't have to make endless phone calls or type information into a tracking form. All customers have to do is click on a simple link to track their orders immediately. It's sweet and simple. This process also provides a marvelous way for companies to drive value from the transactional interface with the customer.

Companies making Mistake #3 just take the order and send the product. That's it. Customers don't know if their product was actually shipped until it shows up at their door. That approach is just bad for business.

Of course, in order to make the superior customer experience work, all of the logistics of distribution must be transparent to your customers. It requires that all internal operations be engineered to run quickly, efficiently, and flawlessly.

1.3.4 Mistake #4: Driving Only for the Point Product

Another mistake companies often make is to drive only for the point product. You order a widget, they sell you a widget, and they ship you a widget. End of story.

Amazon and Dell have brilliantly avoided this mistake by mastering the upsell. Each company continues to offer well-targeted suggestions for additional purchases. Navigate their sites on a regular basis, and you see how they have elevated data mining and customer relationship management to new heights. They know what kinds of things interest you and what kinds of things you are likely to purchase next.

Maximizing your company's success factor has a lot to do with maximizing eyeball time (the amount of time your customer actually spends on your Web site) and analyzing the places that customers are clicking on your site. Companies making the mistake of focusing only on the point product miss golden opportunities to study their customers' surfing and buying behaviors. These behaviors, as we have seen, are ripe areas for offering purchasing suggestions the next time that your customers visit your Web site.

1.3.5 Mistake #5: Your Products in Someone Else's Shopping Basket

First-time firms jumping into the business of selling over the Internet often fall into an unanticipated pit. While designing their Web sites, they establish links to the sites of their business partners or potential suppliers. That's a common practice. The problem occurs when a customer, looking to buy something from the original site, clicks on a link to a business partner's or supplier's site. Unfortunately, their shopping basket doesn't follow them to the new site, and that's a major problem.

What is the result? Your customer sets up a new shopping basket on the site to which you sent them. With just a click of the mouse, your sale has fallen into the shopping basket of another vendor.

The problem can be avoided by designing your site so that the right links are managed in the right way and so that the ultimate transaction is credited to your company. With a superb IT integration effort, sales, logistics, and delivery to the customer can be streamlined to the customer's—and your—greatest satisfaction.

1.3.6 Mistake #6: Foregoing a Customer Usability Study of Your Site

How bad can your Internet site really be? After all, you've spent a small fortune having it designed by a group of people who really seem to know what they're doing. But do they?

It's amazing what you'll discover when you bring a group of potential customers into a focus group and ask them to try to use your site to buy a product or two. Have your designers and your marketing team watch what happens behind the one-way mirrors and videotape the whole process.

Watch how people get lost on your site. You may very well discover that your site isn't as intuitive as your designers lead you to believe.

I'd like to go as far as to suggest placing a piece of duct tape over your designer(s) mouth(s) while your subjects are testing out your site. Sure, it's going to be a blow to their egos to know that their sites weren't as brilliantly conceived as they thought, but, in the long run, this research will pay back great rewards. By the way, the duct tape is entirely optional.

1.4 Exploiting Major Internet Technology Trends

Assuming that your primary goal in reading this book is to put your business on the fast track to profit, how can this best be done? Your best shot at driving new revenue is to better focus on your existing customers by leveraging today's best Internet technologies into your own business operations. These improvements in your methods of operation will generate cold, hard cash, which will fall straight into your (increasingly profitable) bottom line.

For companies like HP and IBM, nearly half of their new profit potential comes from driving greater efficiencies within their own organizations. Up to 40 percent of new profit potential comes from driving greater efficiencies back through their supply chains. Only about 15 percent of new profit potential comes from creating additional revenue opportunities with existing customers.

It's quite an eye-opener when you realize that nearly all of your new profit potential can be realized by improving the way your company does business, and here's the real beauty of this discovery: You can take incremental, extraordinarily powerful steps on this track toward profitability with each of these steps being easily and quickly cost justified.

The payback is often realized within six months to a year on each of those incremental investments. Companies see very rapid payback, coupled with the sequential, logical, and highly visible improvements in the way they operate.

1.4.1 Where to Start Applying the Best Internet Technologies

Consider first the way in which your products get designed. Then, consider the way in which your products get delivered. Although some killer technologies have been available for years, it still surprises me how few companies actually know how to exploit their potential.

Consider the case of so many companies that were manufacturing discrete products back in the late 1980s. These companies were investing in Computer-Aided Design (CAD) machines in record numbers, and they also brought in a lot of numerically controlled machines. The problem was that each numerically controlled machine had its own programming language and its own set of communications requirements. Similarly, the CAD systems had different ways of interacting with each other, and the various CAD systems generally did not transfer information directly to the numerically controlled machines.

These companies faced the formidable challenge of bringing the CAD and Computer-Aided Manufacturing (CAM) environments together. However, bringing computer-aided design and computer-aided manufacturing together in a seamless fashion was one tough nut to crack.

Could CAD drawings be translated into commands given to the CAM machines? Well, one thing was absolutely certain. Someone needed to figure out how to reduce the amount of iterations that you had to do between the two in order to reduce the number of programming mistakes that were being made between the various units. After all, a programming mistake that wasn't discovered until the product was put together, or even worse, when it was out in the customer's hands, could sink a company.

That realization prompted discrete manufacturers to become the first large-scale adopters of Internet technologies to solve their communications problems.

Internet technology bridged these two islands of automation. After the CAD machines and the CAM machines were both speaking the Internet protocol, programmers were able to create a whole new vocabulary of communications between those basic processes. This bridge has worked wonders in the abilities of many companies to reduce the time to market, the overall cost of manufacturing, subsequent warranty costs, personal injury lawsuits, and a myriad of other related costs.

However, even with these irrefutable examples of how applying Internet technologies to business processes can put a company on the fast track to profit, many, many industries out there are still operating in the relative dark ages.

Take, for instance, the publishing industry. This is one of the classic examples of an industry beset by islands of automation that can't communicate with one another. Commercial printers, for example, will bring in a big, shiny, and new press. Very impressive. They'll also have some nifty automation associated with it, but it's not linked into their order management system. It's also not linked into their inventory control system. Therefore, the whole process is out of balance, with enormous amounts of manual steps in between, introducing huge amounts of delay and tons and tons of waste. It's mind-boggling.

More and more of the world's largest publishers are realizing that their very survival depends on making some smart and targeted changes. At HP, for example, we've put some of our best Internet hotshots on a team that serves one of the largest publishers in Europe. The top management team at this company thought they already had an end-to-end automated system in place. Little did they know….

When our team went in and actually talked to the folks on the shop floor, they found out that these people were maintaining manual data in Excel spreadsheets or on written pieces of paper. They were then coming in on the weekends to enter that information into their computer system. Amazing.

What management thought was a real-time reporting system was usually two weeks late, and it was certainly not useful in the day-to-day life of anybody doing the job. Also, keep in mind that every one of these manual transactions was fraught with the opportunity for error. Is it any wonder that the management team wasn't getting the efficiency out of the system that they had put in place?

The difficulty with most organizations is that they operate in isolated department silos. Unless you step back and look at all of these silos with an unbiased eye, it's tough to get the big picture and to understand the urgency of applying Internet technologies to a company's end-to-end operations.

Consider your own company, for example. Take a look at your accounting system. Perhaps you brought in Service Advertising Protocol (SAP), but then what are you using for your physical inventory control? You may have an automated inventory warehouse of some sort, right? Does it link directly into your accounting system? If not, you already have a manual translation step built into your system because someone is going to have to enter inventory data into your accounting spreadsheets by hand, and that can spell t-r-o-u-b-l-e. That's where mistakes often happen.

Traditionally, vendors have built up vertical expertise around certain applications and functional areas of business. When they come in the door, they bring a certain technology with them. However, unless your entire organization is using Internet technologies, it's going to be almost impossible to link one vendor's solutions with another's.

When you take the global view across your entire organization, you will finally discover how to arrive at big breakthroughs in efficiency and organizational effectiveness. Major breakthroughs are enabled through the application of Internet technologies, and, best of all, these kinds of breakthrough projects almost always have a very, very short-term payback.

1.4.2 Two Approaches

When you're ready to start applying Internet technologies to all of your company's business practices, you really have two main choices. You can either take on this challenge by using inside people and resources, or you can look outside your company for the expertise you need.

There's also a hybrid approach, in which you hire a high-end firm to do the integration work on your behalf with your involvement throughout the process.

The integration work will obviously be different today than it was even a decade ago, when our biggest challenge was getting CAD systems to talk to CAM systems. Today, of course, in addition to large computer systems, companies are also equipping their employees with Personal Digital Assistants (PDAs) and new-generation cell phones, in addition to a variety of other gadgets that are not necessarily all Internet enabled. The work of connecting all of these devices, large and small, is not a job for the timid or ill trained.

The good news is that, as the consumer Internet revolution steams forward, more and more companies are beginning to understand the importance of having basic Internet-enabling in all of their products. Believe me, this is going to make the task of creating links much easier over time.

There's also some nifty World Wide Web Consortium (W3C, the main standards body for the Web) work happening around Extensible Markup Language (XML, an extremely simple Web dialect). This is making it much easier to integrate both content and business process and personal information than it's ever been before.

Not to be outdone, things like JavaBeans and .NET are also making application integration easier. These technologies allow companies to link modules and services together that weren't necessarily designed to link in specific ways.

All of these new technologies are in their infancy and have a long road to travel before they can offer a cookie-cutter, point-and-click approach to integration, yet each offers great promise.

1.5 Preparing the Troops

When you are about to embark on major systemic changes within your organization, you are most assuredly going to run into the challenge of preparing your team for the road ahead.

Every generation has its own fights with technology. Years ago, when I was a professor, the PC was just being introduced. I remember many of our senior faculty members were resisting PCs, unlike our junior faculty, who couldn't wait to get their hands on this new technology.

As the senior faculty painfully, and ever so reluctantly, acquiesced before agreeing to try PCs, there was still one last professor who literally would not give up his punch cards. I had one card reader left in the university, and it was costing us a fortune to maintain.

Desperate times call for desperate measures, right? Therefore, I asked to borrow this professor's punch cards. I had somebody run the cards and put them into a computer file on the local network. Then, I put a computer terminal in the professor's office and assigned somebody to hold his hand to get him through this difficult adjustment period. The problem was that this professor still kept his punch cards up on his shelf for security, just in case the tape backups or computers all around him crashed. Change can be difficult.

Of course, today's kids are growing up in an entirely different environment. Kids 20 years ago used to sit in front of their TVs, just like bumps on a log. They didn't move; they hardly blinked. Today's kids will sit in front of a TV, but they expect to interact with it because of video games, computer games, and more.

Today's kids are used to a highly intensive, highly interactive environment. Pity the teachers who try to herd these kids into an unnatural learning environment by requiring that the kids sit still and stay quiet. Unfortunately, it's probably going to take a generation before all of this interactive technology works its way into the classroom.

On the work front, one of the greatest problems we're having with new technology is a direct result of it not having been domesticated before it gets introduced. In other words, the user interfaces are not the least bit intuitive, which inflicts unnatural pain and torture on people in the workplace.

A huge mistake many companies make is trying to make the new business process or system look just like the old one. It is far better to communicate openly to people that major change will be required. It is critically important to communicate the benefits to individuals and to the company of making the change and then ensuring that the delivery team does a great job of making the valuable functions work better than they used to.

It's been a good 10 years since we've had a major breakthrough in computer-user interfaces. We're ripe, rather overripe, for one now, and it will surely speed the course of progress when it arrives.

Consider the cell phone. It has been domesticated, and that is why the cell phone market is five times the size of today's computer market. The technology has been tamed to the point where it is easier to take a cell phone and connect it to the network than it is to deal with a computer on the road.

Therefore, clearly, there is much work yet to be done to domesticate computer technology. However, great benefits can be realized today in the workplace by implementing incremental changes in technologies.

Above all, if you've been chosen to lead this crusade in your company, you must first be very explicit about the benefits that will be gained from the change. Make sure you dig into the problem well enough at the outset of the project so that you can correctly scope out your mission. Then communicate the living daylights out of your mission and the benefits that it will likely yield. This will lessen the pain that change usually inflicts.

Second, you must measure your results before, during, and after the change.

Third, identify people whose professional lives will be most affected, and most improved, by the changes and wire them first. These may be the secretaries who support the executives, for example. These folks will be great cheerleaders for your mission, and I urge you to involve them early and often in the process.

Finally, I think that it is critical to celebrate successes along the way with your team. Set up your mission in multiple stages so that you have natural points at which you can evaluate your progress and celebrate your successes. Rome wasn't built in a day, and, surely, the entire menu of your business practices will not be fully integrated and streamlined overnight either. Therefore, take things in discrete steps and share the glory as successes are realized.

One of the greatest beauties of the Internet is that each of the steps you will be taking can stand alone. This won't be like putting in an SAP system and ripping out the old accounting system. This will involve, literally, taking what you've got, identifying it incrementally along the way, and sequentially working on it, one piece at a time.

By defining the outcomes that you're trying to achieve, you'll be able to do a on-the-spot cost-benefit analysis easily and often. By breaking your mission into incremental steps, you'll give yourself room to make refinements along the way. By creating attainable benchmarks, you'll be laying out a formula whereby breakthroughs are systematically and predictably achieved.

The Internet has had an enormous impact on people. It caused us to think about the use of information technology strategically and how we could use it to run our businesses. Before the Internet, technology was largely focused on the operational side of business, rather than on the strategic side. That is no longer true.

Improving Your Business Scenarios

Technology is a great servant, but it's also a tyrant as a ruler. I've seen so many people treat technology, especially Internet technology, with almost religious fervor. Doing so can lead to several fatal mistakes when people dive into major transformational plays. Therefore, before you make any changes in your current processes, let's examine some mistakes others have made. You have my guarantee that this will save you a lot of time, expense, and headaches.

The first mistake that some people make is to get preoccupied and blindly enamored with new technology. They get so lost in the technology that they start making changes for the sake of change rather than for the business value that change can yield. The second mistake that people make is that they don't study the new technology enough to understand its advantages—and limitations—and, as such, fall into the trap of believing that technology is somehow going to solve all of their basic business problems. This is also a formula for failed technology implementation projects because the objectives of the project are too nebulous to achieve success.

I urge you to take the time to understand any new technology that you are about to embrace and then to define exactly, in terms of business objectives, what you want this technology to do for you. This is how you'll increase your odds of having technology be your faithful and reliable servant.

2.1 The Early Bird Catches the Worm

I'd like to recommend that you begin your journey on the fast track to profit by casting technology in a servant's role. Technology is going to work—and work hard—for you. However, in order to make this happen, you've got to pay the price up front by focusing on the business benefits that you are trying to achieve from the transformation.

Keep in mind that, if you don't inform yourself as to what the technology is capable of doing for you, your competitors will surely inform you of what it's capable of doing for *them*.

When I hear people say that they don't want to be on the leading edge of technology because they don't want to learn the hard way by making the first mistakes, my skin crawls. Trust me. If you're not on the leading edge, you're on the trailing edge, and you're missing the first-mover advantage. This is a big mistake. Companies that enjoy the best long-term, sustainable benefits from technology are those that understand it and apply it wisely, quickly, and effectively in their business scenarios.

I hear a lot of companies say that they don't want to be on the "bleeding" edge of new technology. They'd rather be a more cautious follower than a leader. You might be able to get away with that strategy if you're near the top of the leader board. However, if you're not, with the speed of modern business today, you're probably going to be severely handicapped relative to the competition, and you may never regain your basic business advantages. Although you don't have to be first, you have to be among the first to exploit major new technologies to get the strategic benefit. If you are among the last half, you will be playing catch-up and will discover that what was a strategic advantage for your competitor is now a competitive cost of doing business for you.

Today, Internet families of technology have a broad sweep to them, and their implications are great. Because these technologies have such definitive strategic advantages, you can really enjoy tremendous first-mover advantages if you're quick on your feet to adopt these. With focused, skillful application of these Internet technologies, you'll find that you can greatly improve your business results in record time.

Now, keep in mind that you'll likely have plenty of behind-the-scenes, operational folks who will be deploying this technology for you. You'll know that they've finished their job when you are able to say that the technology is working seamlessly and flawlessly for you.

Beware, however, that plenty of technology professionals exist who will only do half the job that they should, leaving it to your customers, employees, or supply-chain partners to actually make the technology work. Think back to any Web site that you've visited lately, where you've run up against brick walls while navigating. This is an example of how doing half the job of technology implementation can cost your company dearly in terms of lost, angry, and/or frustrated customers. The problems are even worse when you carefully examine how most Internet technologies are actually deployed and managed.

Therefore, my advice to you is to focus on the business benefits that you want to achieve and then to adopt early and implement completely. Don't relent until the business value is actually delivered. What you're really after here is focused, skillful application of the technology to improve your business results.

Finally, it is critical to shut down the activities, systems, and operations that the new processes replace. Too many firms create the new things and fail to prune the trailing edge of old technology. This quickly becomes expensive and unsupportable.

2.2 Checking Your Foundational Business Fundamentals

Checking your foundational business fundamentals begins with having a clear understanding of your market and everything that's happening within it.

Begin by asking these questions:

- What business are we in?
- Is it a rapidly growing market?
- Is this a mature market?
- Are the customers for your products the same customers you've had before, or are they people who are rapidly adopting new products or services of this kind?

- What are the profit margins in the industry?
- How fast do product changes occur in your industry?

Make sure you have a thorough understanding of the basics of the market dynamics in the areas in which you are competing. This is absolutely critical and should be one of your first steps in checking your foundational business fundamentals.

Next, you must take a careful look at all of your production functions:

- Thoroughly examine what's happening around the procurement of products and technologies in your industry.
- Study how products are being delivered today.
- Ask whether some companies out there are more efficient in delivering products or services than you are.
- Examine the innovations that they have adopted.
- Identify weaknesses among your competition that you can exploit or improve upon.
- Completely understand the current state-of-the-art technology because this will provide you with the kind of insight that can give you quite the competitive edge going forward.
- Review your cost structure.
- Focus on your delivery times.
- Find out more about your partners.
- Conduct an overview of your suppliers' businesses.
- Find out more about their profit margins.
- Think through the whole value delivery chain. Skip nothing.

General Electric (GE) is perhaps the best example of a portfolio company that has, over a long period of time, employed a very sophisticated model for understanding its markets and the dynamics within them. It's also done a world-class job of looking for synergistic opportunities across its product lines. As a result, GE has had a very consistent market valuation over a very, very long period of time. This dates back at least 30 years and long before Jack Welch came to power. GE is a world-class example of how a company can benefit by paying extraordinary attention to its business fundamentals across each of its product lines. You'd be hard-pressed to find a company that manages its entire portfolio of businesses, on a short- and long-term basis, better than GE.

What happens when you don't examine your foundational business fundamentals on an ongoing basis? Other smarter and more thorough companies will leave you in the dust. That happened to a number of e-Schwab's competitors, leaving the gate open for Schwab to excel.

Many of these companies thought they could just go on selling securities through financial consultants forever. Making a direct sale to a customer had never seriously crossed their minds. However, soon they realized that they could no longer afford the expensive financial consultant delivery mechanism upon which they based their business models because savvy customers were heading to e-Schwab, which was offering customers dramatically lower transactional costs.

I've seen this happen in company after company and industry after industry. The lesson herein is to check your foundational business fundamentals thoroughly and on an ongoing basis. Benchmark your company against the best-in-class examples out there and be prepared to move quickly and decisively when changes are warranted. If you spend a year or two denying that business fundamentals in your industry are changing, you might never regain your competitive position.

If you don't get your foundational business fundamentals right, you'll likely have a whole set of cascading investments and strategic capabilities that are not going to function well.

2.3 Developing Your Communications Infrastructure

Company after company has discovered that a first-class communications infrastructure is the foundation for business process improvement. Neglecting this fundamental investment causes information systems to be developed to circumvent the limitations of the current infrastructure or to make piecemeal investments in improving portions of the infrastructure. Either way, this results in systems that are inefficient and strategically limited. These problems become more obvious and painful over time. They are also more difficult to undo and then deploy a good infrastructure at a later date.

Developing a great communications infrastructure begins with an examination of the touchpoints your company has with your employees, your customers, and your distribution chain. After you identify where those touchpoints are, you're in an excellent position to identify the kind of communications infrastructure that you'll need in order to reach out to these people in a meaningful way. You may well need to include Internet technologies in this infrastructure, but keep in mind that the Internet is not the answer to all the world's problems. A blend of communications strategies is a more workable scenario for most companies. On the other hand, driving toward the use of Internet protocols on top of the underlying communications infrastructure can make upgrades and the use of new technology more seamless and less expensive.

A classic example is Ford Motor Company, which today has a touchpoint with every single Ford dealer in the country through its high-speed satellite links that operate in both directions. These allow Ford to maintain the parts inventories in the dealerships and also to train, both of which can easily be managed by means of direct video across its satellite infrastructure.

As you know, a number of companies around the world communicate regularly with many dealers. Setting up T1 circuits with all of these dealers would be nearly cost prohibitive. For them, satellite video conferencing is today's alternative from both an effectiveness and a cost standpoint.

If a company tried to duplicate the Ford satellite investment today with land lines, it would undoubtedly cost more and would not give the kind of coverage satellites provide. This is because land lines alone would not be able to get T1 circuits to all the rural dealers that broadcast satellite networks could reach.

You'll find that many global companies today are using a tapestry approach to their communications infrastructure, taking advantage of both satellite communications and DS3, OC3, and T1.

Moreover, the Internet is loaded with all sorts of advantages of its own. For example, the Internet allows companies to reach out to their customers much more aggressively than they might otherwise be able to afford. In addition, these same companies can work with their supply chain through high-speed links, making secure, collaborative design efforts possible.

Whatever type of business you're in, you'll want to focus on three things when developing your communications infrastructure. First, understand what your distribution chain and customer touchpoints look like. From there, you can then develop a communications infrastructure that is most appropriate for your needs. Second, look back at your supply function and develop an infrastructure that's appropriate for it. Finally, thoroughly examine the communications environment that you have in place for your employees. This is key to your overall success and should be a central element in your overall communications infrastructure plan.

You can leverage Internet technologies at any time and through a number of different applications. These technologies offer tremendous benefits in terms of speed and economics, but they should not be used as your exclusive communications infrastructure network.

As time goes on, Internet technologies allow companies to further customize their communications activities. This helps envelop your customers in a seemingly high-touch environment, which could be extremely good for business.

If you don't have the resources within your own company to develop a first-rate communications infrastructure, a number of companies out there can help. For example, American Telephone and Telegraph (AT&T); Microwave Communications, Incorporated (MCI) Worldcom; Qwest; Level 3; and Sprint have done an incredible job, behind the scenes, working with companies to put together coherent, efficient, and effective communications infrastructures. Similarly, in Europe, British Telecom, Koninklijke PTT Nederland (KPN), Deutsche Telecom, and others have great capabilities. Singtel in Singapore, Telstra in Australia, and many companies in Japan also have great capabilities.

Some local exchange carriers are quite good in terms of their ability to set up a communications infrastructure, but, frankly, others have been a bit spotty in their service. Because of this, I think it would be well worth a company's time to talk to one of the major national telecommunications carriers about their costs and architectural capabilities. Unfortunately, small businesses probably won't have this option, but all medium and large businesses should certainly be talking with the major carriers.

I have a word of caution, however. It's possible to spend more money to obtain a worse communications infrastructure than you presently have. State and local governments are notorious for making this mistake, although they do it with the best intentions. They'll say that they want a certain type of network architecture and put it out for competitive bid. However, all they really want is for the carriers' best network engineers to go through a complex bidding process to come up with some sort of a Rube Goldberg kind of network that just happens to match exactly the architecture described by the state or local government.

Few customers understand a carrier's network infrastructure. Latency and bandwidth are the critical design considerations, and these capabilities are not visible to customers in the kind of detail required for network design. Also, most organizations don't do enough Wide Area Network (WAN) design to understand how applications behave in this environment. Finally, every carrier has a different topology, allowing the carrier to maximize the use of its own network infrastructure, rather than leasing capability from other carriers, which usually results in lower overall cost, higher availability, and better overall performance.

Without question, the best procurements are the ones where the network engineers at the major carriers are given a free rein to provide the new communications network. These guys are seasoned professionals. Some have worked with Internet technologies for 10 or 15 years. Among them are former Sprint and MCI engineers who helped build the original Internet, and they know this stuff like the back of their hands.

Let them leave their brains turned on so that they can help you, and you'll end up with a better communications network at a lower cost than your own engineers are likely to devise. Frankly, your own people don't know the network topology as well as they do, nor do they know the kinds of new services and equipment that have been deployed in recent endeavors. In addition, this makes it easier for carriers to do long-term capacity planning. The more flexibility that the carrier has in doing this means the more likely that you are to have capacity when you need it at a price that you can afford.

Therefore, it's critical that, when you hire these carriers, you allow them to do their best work on your behalf in terms of engineering the perfect solution for your company.

There are a few other things that you should consider, not the least of which is the reliability of your new communications infrastructure. Examine this issue from every angle. It can make or break your ability to take the fast track to profit. Remember that poor reliability is most often the result of an applications failure, rather than a network or server hardware failure. Network failures in modern carrier infrastructures usually result in performance degradation before a hard failure occurs. Internet routing protocols were designed from their early inceptions to recover from individual line failures.

Also, one of the most overlooked parts of the network is what we call latency, which is the time that it takes a packet of data to cross a network connection from sender to receiver. If you are not taking full advantage of what your carrier is capable of delivering in its core infrastructure, you may very well end up with router hops, or delays. Hops through an OC192 are not equal to hops through a DS3, so for some high capacity core networks, larger hop counts produce smaller delays overall. Also, IP layer hops may not reveal the underlying MPLS or ATM or FR "hops" so again, lower hop count may be misleading. If you end up with a lot of latency in your network, applications like voice won't work very well, and you'll see jerkiness in some of your video streaming. Beyond that, your email system may not be deployed and functioning properly.

Finally, keep in mind that your communications infrastructure also has implications for application deployment. Your carrier may tell you that, in order to take advantage of its best performance capabilities, you may need to change the way that you have your applications deployed. In fact, it would not be unusual for this to happen. For example, you might have the wrong data centers doing the wrong kinds of applications in the wrong locations given the new infrastructure that's being deployed.

Again, I urge you to allow your carrier to use all of its brainpower to help you put together a coherent network infrastructure, even if that infrastructure requires changes in your application deployment. This allows your company to get peak performance out of your new network. Rather than tying the hands of your carrier, leverage its brainpower instead. You'll be amazed by the astonishing results.

2.4 Organizing, Storing, and Locating Information on the Internet

The first problem with most business information today is that it is poorly organized. You can't get your hands on the information that you need quickly enough. Does this sound familiar?

I've learned in advanced technology development that you understand the problem 10 times better after you've tried to solve it than you did before you started. However, your organization of information typically reflects your first set of understandings of that problem.

If you've incrementally engineered your solution, you'll reach the point where it's almost impossible to add to your information base and to organize it around your initial structure in a manner that makes any kind of sense at all. Most businesses will find that when they begin to explore how they might better organize their information, the results can be quite extraordinary. One nice thing about the Internet is that you can use it to prototype new information architectures rapidly, and you can prototype them, in turn, around major value propositions or value delivery chains.

HP has done a splendid job of using Internet technologies in its imaging and printing systems business. HP makes core formatter boards, basic printing engines, drivers, toner, and so on, and all of these processes are maintained in independent databases. Each process represents a critical path to getting the finished products out the door. Previously, a lot of manual coordination was going on to coordinate all these processes.

Recently, HP has taken advantage of some new Internet technologies that have allowed the company to put together some slick dashboards where all of these processes can be linked together in one place. After getting there, a team leader or a manager can oversee the status of each of these related and interdependent systems. The dashboard contains integrated text and graphics that make organizing, storing, and locating this information a snap.

In sharp contrast, the *old* Internet was a textual beast using http. The big breakthrough came years later when the beast was tamed and technology companies finally could integrate graphic and textual information and could link them all together dynamically.

The same basic concept can be applied to your own information systems. You can take a tremendously complex production system, with all sorts of corollary processes, and, from a top level, link them together in a meaningful, easily accessible fashion.

If you look at the financial services industry, you'll see a number of companies out there that have done a really good job of taking all of their financial offerings and making them available to their customers in a single location on the Web. Fidelity, for example, has done a fine job in this regard. It has created a customercentric view of the accounts and offerings that it has available, and, with the Web, it is seamlessly linked together.

The airlines also have done some terrific work in this area. Up until recently, it was a nightmare for customers to find out whether their plane was on time, make reservations for future flights, or check on their frequent-flyer accounts. Today, unbeknownst to the customers, all that data is maintained on separate systems, but brought together in a single location for their ease and benefit.

Today, the Internet has made so many laborious tasks of yesterday hundreds of times faster, and we, as customers, just take it for granted that the information is just a mouse click away.

That's a very disruptive bit of technology that has arisen from the Internet. Businesses have incorporated rapid prototyping of a new view, a new way of looking at their businesses, and a new way of looking at the way that they serve customers. The results have been lightning quick and tremendously profitable.

2.4.1 Process Automation and Integration

Next, I'd like to suggest that you look beneath the covers after you complete your initial information-integration work and ask yourself what you've learned as a result of this work.

Is it now possible to refine your processes so they are even more user-centric? If the answer is yes, the next steps might seem quite radical, but this is the time when you'll start to get some real value out of your investment. What I have found is that most companies stop short of completing this process. They get some undeniable value out of the first phase of their information-integration work, but they're getting only 20 to 30 percent of what they could wring out of those new systems. How can they capture the remaining 70 to 80 percent?

Let's say you believe you now have your information organized to a state of near perfection. Then, you identify two or three databases that get hit for every transaction. Hmmm. Should you create a larger, more integrated database, or should you maintain bits and pieces of customer information?

The good news is that, if you've designed your new information systems from the Web in, as opposed to designing them from the systems out, you're going to be leaps and bounds ahead of the pack when you start to think about fine-tuning your systems so that new sources of profitability can be squeezed out of your operations.

During the redesign phase, you can look at your actual system uses and begin to predict their value because you'll have some very helpful prototypes at your disposal. Even if your operating systems are functioning well, you still should view these as prototypes. You'll be able to use them to judge what the traffic is likely to be on your various systems and where the big repositories of data fit today.

From there, you can go back to your network design and determine if your systems are allowing your data to sit closer to the customer. You might decide that you should maintain replicas of the data out on the frontend. Replicas are quite often used for security purposes. These replicas require a high-transaction volume system.

Behind the firewall, you can keep a low-volume system with high integrity built into it. This system carries with it some pretty profound implications for the way you relocate data.

Similarly, you may choose to put some of your internal corporate data in the network infrastructure, rather than within the data centers that you have in your enterprise. This can be done because the interactions among those systems may be faster and closer, and the average user is going to come into that system more as a consumer, albeit across your own internal network infrastructure.

Again, for security and other reasons, you should separate the public side and the internal, corporate side with firewalls. However, they should be run on an identical network infrastructure in order to facilitate speed and ease of use.

A lot of companies discover that, after they think through this entire process, they almost always will redeploy their servers in different locations within the company. Quite often, companies have deployed their data close to where the data was originally developed. However, with a rationalized network infrastructure, these same companies may want to redeploy their data to reflect its usage pattern, rather than its development pattern.

It's perfectly acceptable to store your data away from the people who are generating it. This causes a major shift in the way an IT infrastructure is set up, but can give companies the ability to outsource in ways they couldn't before. This added flexibility could improve your bottom line in a very significant fashion.

2.5 Integrating Your Design and Manufacturing Processes

There's been a quiet revolution that's been going on behind the scenes lately, which has allowed design and manufacturing processes to be intertwined with symphonic precision. This is an area in which the industry has shifted radically in the last five to seven years, and a lot of folks don't realize the scope or magnitude of these changes.

Five years ago, if you wanted to bring a product to market, you would do the design internally and then take it out to a contract manufacturing company, and it would bid on doing the actual manufacturing work for you. You might have several contract manufacturers build separate components for you, and your company would do the final assembly. Today, in many cases, large design-and-manufacturing companies do the initial design work for you, or the finished product design work, or both. They can also do the manufacturing work for you. They may work with five or six subcontractors, or maybe more. A whole network of these design and manufacturing conglomerates are out there today.

This has created a major shift in design and manufacturing processes. This capability would not have been possible without using a solid Internet foundation. What I have found is that many companies have not yet recognized that this shift has occurred. They're continuing to invest in their own design capabilities, or, worse yet, they do the initial design and then go out to these companies and have the product redesigned. This duplication of effort can prove to be a costly error.

An inadvertent redundancy in your supply chain can preclude your company from taking the fast track to profit. Understanding that a paradigm shift has taken place in design and manufacturing processes and taking advantage of this major shift can yield startling benefits in extremely short order.

Let's say you want to get a product out there with a fabulous user-centered design. However, your company doesn't have all of the capabilities in-house to create this product and get it out the door. You now have the ability to find those needed skills quickly and easily by tapping into a full network of provisioning companies.

Also—and here's a very important consideration—the scale of business you need to be successful today is much smaller than it used to be.

Because you have these big provisioning companies at your disposal, they can procure the components and can leverage their size, bringing greater profit opportunities to your company.

It used to be that when you would build a product in-house, you were at an immediate cost disadvantage because you couldn't get the cost of parts at the lower price than your larger competitors. You had to produce higher-priced products to cover your higher manufacturing costs, but this is no longer true. Today, you can scale your business at your discretion, and your time to market is shorter than it's ever been.

Additionally, the worldwide logistics that are associated with getting your product to market are dramatically different because outsourcing companies have global manufacturing partners that can produce your products closer to your points of sale than ever before. This means less inventory risk for your company, which translates into greater profit potential.

FAST TRACK TO PROFIT TIP

I'd like to state this as clearly as I can:

You're not being realistic if you don't thoroughly examine the full design and manufacturing cycle of your business scenario because therein major profit opportunities abound. My experience at HP, International Business Machines (IBM), and other companies has led me to believe that probably 45 to 50 percent of the opportunity to exploit the world's best Internet technologies can be found in the realm of design and manufacturing or the way in which you create and deliver services. That's the largest single block of business value at your immediate disposal.

Of course, if you haven't first defined your customers and your markets very well, you could end up with a warehouse full of things that nobody wants. Therefore, focus first on the needs of your customers, because that's your lifeline. Then, take a long, hard look at your design and manufacturing processes. You'll be so glad you did.

2.6 Focusing on Customer and Tech Support

In the late 80s and early 90s, a whole host of companies was selling things, not on the Internet, but for the Internet. They were selling things to get the Internet started, and one of those things they were selling was customer and tech support.

Cisco Systems was one company that really led the market when it came to Internet-driven customer and tech support. It was making it easy for its customers to find out information about its products online. Cisco also was leading the way in providing easy Internet downloads of patches and fixes, and its technologies were enabling users to set up online communities where the users could support each other.

I just don't see companies doing that anymore. It was, you know, such a powerful thing to do in the early days of the Internet because none of this technology worked extremely well. You also had a pretty small user community that had personally invested a lot in this new technology, and, quite often, the users themselves were the best sources of tech support.

Today, many kinds of products and services would benefit greatly from building user communities on the Internet. It's unfortunate, I think, that we've reached an era where companies have focused all of their efforts on the outbound side of customer and tech support and haven't focused on building communities of their users. Of course, there is the rare exception to this rule, most notably illustrated by the whole Linux phenomenon. Linux was almost entirely user developed, and it is basically all user supported.

My feeling is that somewhere between Linux and the average company model of customer and tech support lies a realm of great possibility for major improvements through the building of user communities. This won't be just a matter of pulling information online, but rather of building a community of people who are interested in a particular product or technology, or both. Without question, this thought causes a considerable amount of culture shock for some companies because many of them don't want to admit that they've ever created a product that has had a problem.

This also will require that companies be willing to be honest with their customers and let them know that they have a few warts and where those warts are. In addition—scare of all scares—companies will have to let their customers talk to one another about their products and their weaknesses.

This might be a little easier to handle if you consider this: I have yet to see a perfect product from any company.

Therefore, we just need to realize that we're living in an imperfect world, and all companies and all products have their warts and their problems. You're far better off being honest and frank about them and letting your customers talk about them in an open forum.

That being said, let me emphasize how important it will be to have your own folks monitor these user communities. These forums can be one of the greatest sources of new product ideas, new service models, and all sorts of other wonderful ideas about how to improve your existing products.

You'd be ill advised just to set up these communities and let them go off on their own paths. You must be publicly visible in the user communities and monitor them with due diligence. There is indeed an art form associated with doing this. Good customer and tech support people are really skillful at guiding an entire community toward good information and, at the same, harvesting that community information for deeper insights about the products and technologies that they are offering.

Start by being frank about your product and its deficiencies. Lose your aura of arrogance. This is what IBM has done, to great advantage. Years ago, IBM was viewed as extraordinarily arrogant, and folks thought that it didn't care about its customers one bit. Then, a cultural shift occurred in the way that IBM handled customer and tech support, and profits began to skyrocket.

Today, Microsoft has the horrible reputation of being arrogant. That bad rep stems mostly from Microsoft's poor customer and tech support. It seems as if the only time you ever get to speak to an actual person at Microsoft is when they want to sell you an upgrade—not good.

Openness and frankness are keys to building credibility with your customers. Couple this with an aggressive harvesting of ideas from your customers, and you'll find your prospects of financial growth greatly improved.

Keep in mind that customers care a lot more about things when they feel like they've been a part of the development process. Most customers believe that they don't have much of a prayer of actually impacting the design of a product personally, but just the fact that they have been able to voice their opinions can be tremendously helpful. I've seen countless customers cheering for a company's success just because those companies were so responsive to their issues and needs.

Never underestimate the value of human interaction. Wherever you do business around the globe, most people prefer to have long-term relationships with trusted suppliers.

The problem is that, with today's commodity technology and its very low margins, the old, traditional face-to-face model of customer and tech support doesn't work very well, economically speaking. The telephony model even has its problems.

However, by using the Internet, it is possible for companies to interact effectively and efficiently with communities of customers, rather than interacting with individuals. Now, this is not to say that companies shouldn't personalize their communications with individuals. Some terrific personalization tools are available today. It is possible, however, through Internet communities, for companies to put the personal touch of human beings into their interactions with their customers in a manner that is profitable, from any angle.

2.7 Selling Gizmos, Gadgets, and Intangibles

2.7.1 Over the Web

You know the story in Hollywood. You come out with a megahit, and, all of a sudden, everyone wants a sequel. Well, that's the same thing that happened with the Internet when everyone saw that Amazon.com was selling a ton of books over the Internet.

Before that time, people hadn't really thought that you could sell books over the Internet. After all, books tend to be fairly low-cost items, and millions of books are out there. Book lovers would never buy books over the Internet, it was thought, because they would want to browse in bookstores and flip through the pages and feel the bindings, wouldn't they? There is that whole tactile response thing, and there are fantastic places like Borders that have done a great job of creating entire customer experiences and environments around books and bookshelves and hot cocoa and cushy chairs.

Well, we all know that, in the midst of the whole Borders book experience, the Internet happened and then Amazon hit. It just sent shockwaves throughout the book industry. Actually, it sent shockwaves throughout planet Earth.

Suddenly, everybody's brain got switched on.

We all said, "Gee, if Amazon can sell books over the Internet, maybe we can sell our gizmos and gadgets over the Internet, too."

Meanwhile, Amazon got the clever idea that it, too, could sell more than books over the Internet. Why, it could sell anything over the Internet, couldn't it?

Whoa, Nelly!!

It didn't take long before Amazon realized that, after it started selling things other than books on its site, it wasn't able to put the same logistics behind the scenes as it had done with books alone. Ever since then, Amazon has been challenged on issues of profitability.

I think that, if Amazon had just stuck to books, they probably could have had a profitable business, pretty darn fast. However, Amazon, like so many Hollywood producers, just couldn't resist the urge to make that sequel. It felt it was in a virtual arms race to move into all those other markets, right off the bat.

Suddenly, everybody was trying to sell furniture online, automobiles online, airplanes online, groceries online, and just about everything else you could possibly imagine. And companies that staked their entire futures on selling their gizmos and gadgets over the Internet were going belly up. What happened?

Well, the biggest mistake that I've seen is that people weren't calibrating the correct balance between the physical and electronic universes. They were forgetting that the Internet works best when you have specialized things to sell in a widely distributed market.

Take the example of specialty foods. My wife and I are fluent Dutch speakers. Try as we might, we just haven't been able to find Dutch food in our hometown of Boise, Idaho. Big problem.

As far as we've been able to determine, the nearest Dutch specialty food store is in California or Utah. Therefore, our next best option is to find our favorite culinary treats on the Internet. Of course, we expect to pay a premium price for some of these ethnic foods, especially if they're authentically imported, so that's what we do. From the Internet to our mouths comes some of the greatest Dutch food in the world.

This business model works well because someone came up with the correct fiscal balance between the physical and the electronic universes.

It didn't work with HomeGrocer.com because someone forgot to do the math. First of all, the grocery business is an extremely low-margin business. When you add home delivery costs to that structure, it made it almost impossible to make money. From a customer's point of view, it took two hours to go online and click on every single grocery item you needed for the week, and then you had to wait until the next day to have your groceries delivered. Instead, you could take 45 minutes to hop in the car, drive down the street, just get what you needed, and come home. No contest.

However, you can't do that with Dutch food in Boise, Idaho, ergo, the Internet.

You don't believe me?

Consider this. There's a company down in Durham, North Carolina, called the Tuba Exchange. The guy who dreamed this up probably sells half of all the tubas sold in the United States. Want to buy a tuba in Boise? Well, there are a couple of music stores in town, but tubas are specialty items, just like that Dutch food my wife and I love so much. You can buy sheet music in Boise and guitars and picks. However, if your pleasure is tubas, you're out of luck. They just don't carry them in their limited inventories. Imagine that!

So, to the rescue, comes this guy in Durham, with his Tuba Exchange. He sells 250 tubas a week. In fact, he's developed a national and international market for tubas, and the Internet has been his passageway to remarkable levels of success and profitability.

To top it all off, this guy doesn't even sell his tubas directly from his Web site. You can scan his site to read all about the various attributes of the tubas he has in stock, but, when you want to place an order, you have to call him on the phone. And wonder of wonders, he's a tremendous personal sales guy because he knows tubas like nobody else in the country, and he has anything you want in his inventory today. No waiting. He's there to serve.

Put that in your tuba and blow on it!

The lesson here is that, for some specialty items, the Internet can be a pretty powerful tool for doing business in situations where the efficiencies and the volumes are not necessarily huge.

However, a lot of companies still haven't thought through these issues fully enough. For example, Furniture.com was a startup that fizzled out in a hurry. It thought selling furniture over the Internet was an outstanding idea. The problem was that furniture is big and bulky and hard to ship. And there's no customer service on the receiving end. And when furniture was getting dinged or broken in transit, customers were fuming because no one was there to help fix the problem. And then there's the problem of shipping costs.

And, Furniture.com made delivery promises it couldn't keep, leaving customers frustrated as they waited and waited for their deliveries. Need I say more?

The Internet just seemed like such fertile ground, and people were just going crazy trying to use it to sell all sorts of small and large gizmos and gadgets. Then fraud started to permeate the sales model, and, all of a sudden, the Federal Trade Commission had its hands full trying to sort out all sorts of national and international Internet scams and schemes. This really pressed the resources of law enforcement almost overnight. Luckily, these issues are now at a manageable stage for law enforcement.

So, take a deep breath, and, before you dive into the realm of selling gizmos, gadgets, and intangibles over the Internet, consider the manageability factor of your business venture. It will be time well spent.

2.8 Reengineering the Way You Do Business

The foundation for any reengineering of the way you do business ought to be a complete focus on the value you're delivering to your customer. Beware of the mistake so many of the dot.com-era people made when they focused only on the value that they wanted their customers to give them, not on the value they wanted to give to their customers. They got it backward, and they paid dearly for their mistakes.

Ask yourself these questions:

- What kind of relationship do I want with my customers?
- How can I deepen and strengthen that relationship?
- How do I add long-term value to my relationship with my customers?
- How do I make my products and services more valuable to my customers?
- How do I surround my customers with offerings and information to make it easy for them to take advantage of new opportunities?
- Is there a Web-delivery paradigm that makes sense for my business?

Take the tuba guy. He puts out a newsletter, an actual, physical newsletter. He does workshops and seminars all over the country. He works with professional tuba players in most of the world's great symphony orchestras, and he has a Web site. He really understands his value proposition, and he has a pretty complete set of delivery mechanisms. He has a scale of business that nobody else in the tuba industry has because he's a one-of-a-kind specialist. To top it all off, the tuba guy really has expertise. He's a phenomenal musician himself.

Sometimes the best high-tech lessons can be found in the most unusual places. That's music to my ears.

CHAPTER 3

Reengineering the U.S. Auto Industry: DaimlerChrysler, Ford, and General Motors (GM)

"**I** have found that higher wages do not mean increased costs, and if our material prices go too high, we will start making our own. We are making a part of everything we use and from the nucleus can readily expand to take care of any or all of our requirements if necessary."

So said automotive pioneer Henry Ford in the April 1934 issue of *Ford News*.

Today, approximately 60,000 companies around the globe supply Ford Motor Company with parts and services. 60,000!

Aaah! The best-laid plans of mice and men....

The very survival of the U.S. auto industry back in the 1980s and 1990s was dependent upon a major paradigm shift. The changes that occurred during this period were dramatic and striking. A fundamental shift occurred in the entire structure of the automobile industry and the way that companies had done business previously. This is a story from which much insight can be gained.

3.1 Change or Permanently Run out of Gas

Back in the 1980s, vertical integration was the dominant logic around which the U.S. auto industry was organized. For example, Ford Motor Company actually manufactured its own steel for the cars it built. In fact, its steel plant was right next door to the plant in which Ford was making its cars. True to Henry Ford's original vision, Ford Motor Company was one of the world's most vertically integrated automotive manufacturers.

In fact, most of the U.S. auto industry in the 1980s was structured in a similar manner. Ford, GM, and Chrysler all were manufacturing most of their own parts.

The Japanese auto industry, on the other hand, had structured itself entirely differently than the U.S. auto industry. Because of its limited geographic area and its denser population, Japanese automakers were forced into a just-in-time business model. They were buying just the parts they needed and just when they needed them—from outside suppliers. As a result, the Japanese auto industry was flourishing, and the U.S. auto industry was beginning a frightening downward spiral, from which no apparent end was in sight.

However, during this time of extreme upheaval and uncertainty in the U.S. auto industry, the industry found a way to conduct a massive—and massively successful—restructuring of the way it designed, manufactured, and marketed its products. At the heart of this exciting restructuring effort was Internet technology. Of course, this was not the consumer Internet. It was the use of Internet technology in a limited way, within the boundaries of the corporation, to solve specific problems, and the payback was immediate.

It's true that, in the United States, we still have many of the same logistics problems that we've always had, and it's also the case that Japanese automakers do not have these problems. However, by exploiting some of the world's best Internet technologies, the U.S. automakers have been able to save their companies and thrive once again in a most impressive fashion.

Central to the problems that U.S. automakers faced in the 1980s was the fact that they were heavily vertically integrated. They owned the parts manufacturers they used, which caused an economic drain on them, and that would soon bury them in debt.

At the same time, the mid-1980s saw a huge struggle to get robotics in place. U.S. automakers weren't nearly as productive as their Japanese counterparts, due in large part to their slow integration of robotic technology. These numerically controlled machines were seen as an answer to the dramatically higher labor costs in the United States.

In addition, the U.S. automotive industry was suffering from some very visible quality problems. Skyrocketing labor costs and serious quality issues necessitated the rapid transition from manual labor to robotic labor in the U.S. auto industry.

Interestingly, if you look at a complex process such as automobile assembly, it's not something that you can program into a computer and have it produce an optimal shop layout for you. It's one of those things in which you must do sequential simulation of modeling and a fair amount of practical work on the shop floor. It's a delicate balance.

The U.S. automakers were not too proud to seek the counsel of their Japanese counterparts during this time of crisis. Out of the mid-1980s sprang a number of joint ventures between U.S. and Japanese automakers. One classic example can be found in the Toyota-Chevrolet plant in California, which affectionately became known as the Chevyota plant. There they produced the Chevy Nova and then the Toyota Corolla.

Ford also was getting into this game by making a heavy investment in Mazda. Ford started an assembly plant in Flat Rock, Michigan, where Mazdas were made. This joint venture opened doors to new ideas for Ford, just as the Chevyota plant provided a learning experience for the Chevrolet team.

Chrysler, not to be left behind, partnered with Mitsubishi.

Basically, what you had was a new set of joint ventures springing up among U.S. auto companies and their Japanese counterparts. During this time, the U.S. automakers learned everything they could about Japanese automaking techniques. From these experiences, the U.S. auto industry recognized that there was a better way to build things. Yet, even though much was learned from Japanese techniques, it was still apparent that both U.S. and Japanese auto manufacturers were struggling with the integration between their computerized design machines and their computerized manufacturing facilities.

When these companies designed a machine, they would then have to translate that design into numerically controlled codes for the robotics to work. This was a major and costly effort, and it seemed as if every robotics machine had its own proprietary communications language. On top of that, the CAD machines had their own proprietary formats for their design drawings.

The design and manufacturing landscape was ripe for change, and that's exactly what occurred in the mid-1980s through the early 1990s.

3.2 Chrysler Ignites in Astonishing Ways

This voyage was not characterized by clear sailing by any means. Take the example of Chrysler. It was on the brink of bankruptcy. Its business models were an unmitigated disaster. Its ability to take a design and bring it to market was just about the worst in the industry. Chrysler had enormous problems with integrating designs into computerized manufacturing machines.

Those problems, along with a host of others, nearly sank Chrysler. That's when the U.S. bailout of Chrysler occurred. This wasn't the typical bailout, though. It was more of a safety net that Chrysler could use against the loans it needed to reengineer itself.

The amazing thing was that Chrysler paid off its U.S. guaranteed loans in record time. Why? Chrysler felt the urgency to change by adopting more industry-standard practices. It was a clear case of sink or swim, and Chrysler won the race.

Under the leadership of Lee Iacocca, Chrysler broke all records in terms of first getting rid of its own proprietary design software and then bringing in industry-standard software that the aerospace industry had been using for some time.

Chrysler focused relentlessly on automating every step of its design and manufacturing processes. In doing so, Chrysler was able to eliminate massive costs in its production processes.

And, lo and behold, out of these darkest days, Chrysler emerged as the premiere auto company in the United States, really shaking up the market with how fast it was able to create new products and bring them to market.

During those days, Chrysler really felt like IBM came in and saved their bacon with that reengineering. Jerry York, who had been the Chief Financial Officer (CFO) at Chrysler, had moved to IBM to be the CFO there. There were some strong and deep ties between those two companies, and the level of mutual trust was enormous.

Chrysler also was enjoying the temporary labor advantage it got from the United Auto Workers. Although this was a cost advantage that the other automakers didn't enjoy, it quickly disappeared after Chrysler began turning a profit.

However, there was clearly a sustainable level of efficiency that Chrysler generated during this period of time because of its aggressive adoption of Internet technologies and automation. Much credit goes to Lee Iacocca and his team, along with the folks who were supplying this Internet technology to Chrysler.

A tremendous marketing effort went on during this time as well. Lee Iacocca could be seen on TV talking about the reengineering efforts at Chrysler and about the tremendously innovative products that were the result of these endeavors. New products were being introduced at a breathtaking pace, and the buying public was hearing about them from the Iacocca himself in a series of long-running television spots. It was pretty darn impressive.

Equally impressive, but not as visible to customers, was the introduction of Chrysler's 1998 Concorde. This was the first automobile that employed a totally paperless design cycle. The product was developed, tested, and validated on the computer: no paper drawings and no clay models. Nothing was used but electronic design, testing, and validation. How remarkable was this achievement? The Concorde won the Power & Associates highest rating for a premium midsize car in 1998. This was a big year for Chrysler in another way, too. It was the year in which Chrysler merged with Daimler-Benz. Overnight, the new company, DaimlerChrysler, became a world leader in transportation.

From the proudest days of Walter P. Chrysler's life, when in 1924 he introduced his first car—the Chrysler Six—to six decades later when Chrysler Chairman Lee Iacocca introduced the new K-cars, to today, when retro innovations like the PT Cruiser are capturing the imaginations of consumers everywhere, Chrysler has been a company to watch.

And Ford and GM were—and are—watching intently.

I should stress that both Chrysler and Daimler-Benz focused on a design-centered revolution while Ford and GM focused more on a supply-chain revolution. Both succeeded extremely well. Additionally, GM has been pioneering a communications-centered revolution with its OnStar technology.

3.3 Ford and GM Hop on Board the Internet Express

Ford and GM had a different set of problems in the mid 1980s caused primarily because they were so vertically integrated. By virtue of its smaller size, Chrysler hadn't been able to realize the level of vertical integration that Ford and GM had achieved.

Those lumbering giants, Ford and GM, were struggling with the enormous problems that they had created by virtue of their dependence on vertical integration. This made it very hard for them to move rapidly and to keep up with the likes of many Japanese and German automakers, and Chrysler for that matter.

Meanwhile, across the pond, traditional European manufacturers were going through some of the same struggles that were besetting Ford and GM. Daimler-Benz, for example, was producing cars that weren't considered innovative. It also had a cost structure that was out of control. It was rapidly being priced out of the U.S. market.

In addition, Volkswagen was going through its own turmoil.

However, even during this period of tremendous upheaval, Ford and GM were able to focus on releasing themselves from the bondage of vertical integration. How did they do it?

On May 22, 1923, Henry Ford remarked in *Ford News*: "Progress consists in a number of related things changing together for the better." How prophetic his words were, especially in the 1980s, when a number of related things were able to change in major ways at Ford and GM.

First of all, Ford and GM spun out their parts operations. After they did this, their parts operations were able to supply a broader range of customers throughout the auto industry, and, as a result, they became profitable for the first time. They began, and continue today, to sell parts to Japanese and European manufacturers, as well as to their traditional, internal U.S. customers.

That was what put them on the fast track to profit.

All of a sudden, Ford and GM were enjoying a new state of nimbleness. However, this was just the beginning of the process by which Ford and GM reengineered the way they did business. Next up, each company developed extraordinary avenues of communication and collaboration with design houses. On top of that, they created extraordinarily tight integration with their manufacturing processes.

Moreover, Ford and GM also were focusing on the larger issue of supply chain logistics. Their focus on just-in-time delivery of inventories made for greater profitability and growth.

3.4 Ford's Unique Set of Road Hazards

Ford also had a set of problems all its own, having to do with the quality of the components being built into its cars. In addition, Ford had enormous factory execution problems. How could Ford possibly ensure end-to-end quality while it was taking its vertical integration architecture apart?

The only way to achieve Ford's hugely ambitious goals was to have a complete and relentless focus on the reengineering of its supply chain, coupled with a complete and relentless focus on what was happening on its factory floor. This passion and dedication were what gave Ford's employees the strength and the momentum to make it through the 1980s and into the 1990s.

Remember their slogan, "Quality is Job 1"? These were words to live by, and grow by, at Ford.

Witness the phenomenon in the 1990s, when Ford acquired premium brands, including Jaguar and Volvo. Since Ford acquired these two companies, the quality of each of these brands has improved. A decade ago, you never would have thought that could be possible, given Ford's recent quality track record.

Ford has dramatically turned a weakness into a strength. Credit goes to the management team at Ford and the IT folks working behind the scenes. In addition to the enormous quality strides Ford has made, it also has done a stellar job of building a dealer network that has allowed it to manage parts in highly efficient, new ways. Great Internet technologies have been exploited in these efforts.

The turnaround in Jaguar and Volvo has been remarkable as well. Both have shown dramatic improvements in their cost structures and improvements in their overall product quality.

3.5 GM Navigates the Bumpy Road Ahead

GM has an interesting story to tell as well. Back in the mid-1980s, GM acquired Electronic Data Systems (EDS) and subsequently moved 100,000 EDS employees to Detroit to help reengineer its business. At the same time,

GM also acquired some of the Hughes Aircraft properties. Those were two interesting acquisitions that yielded some very promising GM technologies.

GM acquired EDS and parts of Hughes to help it manage its broad product line and lagging design problems. In very short order, the newly acquired EDS and Hughes people infused GM with a new spirit and a new urgency to adopt more industry-standard technologies and techniques.

Many folks joked about the odd marriage between GM and EDS. After all, the story goes, the GM people were the ones wearing the beards and the sandals, and the EDS people were the ones wearing the business suits.

They were strange bedfellows, indeed, not to mention the fair amount of culture shock that accompanied this marriage. However, out of this acquisition grew a new and utterly impressive capability by GM to produce cars based upon solid technology-centered engineering. Even with the new suits running around, GM was still able to keep some of its innovative IT culture from the past. There's not a single sign of innovation being stamped out at GM; everything that worked before the acquisition remains intact today. A new sense of professionalism permeates throughout GM these days.

Innovative leadership and the introduction of Internet technologies throughout all of GM's processes have led to some very impressive breakthroughs, including its new OnStar system and the GM Global Positioning System (GPS) system, both of which are vastly superior to anything its competition has introduced.

The folks at GM are living on the edge of technology. GM now brings IT right into the vehicles it builds better than any of its competitors.

GM, as the largest U.S. automaker, also had its set of vertical integration issues, albeit not as severe as those experienced at Ford. Over time, GM has been able to spin out its parts businesses and, in doing such, has increased its profit potential.

After GM overcame the cultural challenges it faced by bringing in the EDS folks, it was well on its way to a new era. That era is now in full bloom and is characterized by GM's ability to incorporate new technologies rapidly into its business practices, resulting in products that are innovative, well built, and thoroughly tested.

3.6 Exploiting Internet Technologies in the U.S. Auto Industry

Exploiting Internet technologies has been fundamental to the reengineering of the U.S. auto industry. Had it not been for these efforts, especially in the areas of CAD/CAM, it is unlikely that the U.S. auto industry would have been able to survive.

How dramatic was the use of Internet technologies by the U.S. auto industry? Well, in the late 1980s, this industry was probably the single largest commercial customer for Internet technologies. In fact, the U.S. auto industry was a good five to six years ahead of the rest of the world. Only the aerospace industry showed early interest in these technologies and only after it saw the radical improvements being enjoyed by the auto industry. The auto industry was using Internet technologies in all of its design and manufacturing processes, as well as in its fundamental business processes.

Back in the early 1980s, GM had teamed with GE and several other companies to start a consortium called the Manufacturing Automation Protocol/Technical Office Protocol (MAPTOP). The existence of MAPTOP grew out of a general frustration with equipment and computer suppliers in the industry. MAPTOP felt that all of these individual suppliers were providing propriety interfaces that made it nearly impossible to succeed in a complex manufacturing environment.

These users banded together to form the MAPTOP Consortium so that they could develop standards and monitor their suppliers' compliance with these standards. Needless to say, this did shake up supply-chain manufacturers in quite a significant way.

By the late 1980s, however, the MAPTOP Consortium discovered the Internet. Much to their delight, the Internet was already out there, and it worked. Sure enough, Internet technologies would be a lot easier to implement than the heavyweight options the MAPTOP folks were considering on their own.

That's how an enthusiastic embracing of Internet technologies by the members of the MAPTOP Consortium came to be. In fact, the auto industry rapidly became the single largest market for the fledgling Internet technology companies and drove much of its growth through the mid-1990s. It would not be an overstatement to say that, without the early adopters in the auto industry, the Internet revolution could not have happened. This industry provided practical problems for the Internet technology community to solve, sales to fuel development of the companies, and high-quality customers to help improve the quality and usability of the technologies. This is one of the great untold stories of Internet history.

It wasn't just communications technology that benefited from the Internet revolution. It also was the UNIX operating system in use in CAD applications, which were the powerful database systems that contained the design and business information. All of this was carefully reengineered to work together using Internet technologies. Folks in the auto industry relentlessly drove their technology suppliers to do the right thing—to reengineer their products around open industry standards that worked.

The early adoption of Internet technologies among automakers laid the foundation for a dramatic restructuring of the industry, and it made it feasible for the industry to build some sustainable competitive advantages that it was able to exploit vigorously during a 10- to 12-year period.

During that time, the U.S. auto industry was able to enjoy dramatic cost savings. Productivity gains during that period skyrocketed. This was remarkable because we were looking at a mature industry going into the late 1980s. This was an industry that was in deep financial trouble. It was an industry that was losing market share on a worldwide basis. It was an industry trying to feed customers unexciting, monolithic designs, and it was an industry characterized by huge labor costs and labor turmoil. On top of these issues, the automotive industry had enormous quality problems with which to deal.

It's difficult to overstate the critical role Internet technologies played in the resurgence of the U.S. auto industry in the mid-1980s and 1990s. These technologies paved the way for a more open kind of communication and a more modular set of architectures with more industry standard tools.

I don't want to discount the hard work and leadership of the executive teams at Ford, GM, and Chrysler, or their IT teams. They had a great record of incredible teamwork inside each of those companies, and together they delivered amazing value during a ten-year period. However, without the Internet technology foundation, I don't think it would have been possible to accomplish the revolution they so masterfully achieved. When you couple that accomplishment with great people, focusing hard on the business values they were going to deliver, an unbeatable combination arose. However, it took great courage to be early adopters of the new Internet technology, and this courage was rewarded with an unbeatable synergy that arose among people and the Internet.

Today, the technology used in designing, manufacturing, and marketing cars in the U.S. has increased dramatically and has led to a resurgence in the auto industry. Innovation abounds throughout the industry today. Because of their remarkable reengineering accomplishments and their improved product-delivery chain, U.S. automakers have done an extraordinary job of improving their sustained profitability.

The auto industry was one of the first manufacturers to put its product specifications online. In the 1990s, the automakers were shipping diskettes with simulators on them, allowing customers to test drive their cars online and to try out the new buttons and other dashboard features. This wasn't their only gambit on their fast tract to profitability.

Dealer networks also have been restructured. Dealer services can now be accessed online, and intermediary Web sites like Autobytel are able to provide additional services to customers.

However, things are not static in this vibrant industry. The channel is shifting rapidly. A decade ago, smaller, independent dealers served most of the U.S. consumer market for automobiles. Today, we're seeing more and more multistate megadealers popping up. This has lead to a much more concentrated distribution channel than existed a decade ago. One wonders how the U.S. auto industry plans to develop a more personal and direct relationship with its customers in the future, thereby ensuring long-term brand loyalty and customer satisfaction. It's a safe bet to assume that Internet technologies will figure heavily into that equation as we move forward in the 21st century.

Looking back over the last decade or so, I would be hard pressed to find another industry, except for perhaps the utility industry, that has gone through as much structural change as the auto industry. So very little of its success would have been possible if it were not for the early adoption of Internet technologies by the big three automakers.

3.7 A Forward View

Considering the state of the U.S. auto industry in the 1980s and 1990s, it's very clear that the industry has grown much stronger, despite a weakening economy. Part of that success is due to the remarkable way in which the U.S. auto industry reengineered itself. Of course, part of its success can also be traced to low interest rates. However, even with very tough challenges to overcome, including the Ford Explorer tire problem, this industry is strong and getting stronger. A decade ago, such a problem could have ruined Ford.

Today, these companies have the wherewithal to be able to endure all sorts of challenges—and in today's economy, there are many—and yet continue to move forward. I think it's a real testament to the intensity and vigor of the executive teams and the IT teams at those companies and the kind of miracles they've accomplished during the last decade.

It's not a glamorous story, but it is an important one. The amount of money that these companies invested in their reengineering efforts was enormous, and the business advantages of doing so created sustainable economic advantages that are just incredible.

Consider one of the nicest features of the Daimler-Benz/Chrysler merger. Obviously, there were culture shock issues to overcome when these two companies merged, but these companies came together with a common technology base. During the 1980s and 1990s, both companies pretty much kicked their individually written design software out the window and instead adopted industry-standard software. They both adopted a very similar set of processes for designing and producing cars.

That made the integration of these two powerhouses a lot easier.

Internet technologies also came to the rescue when Chrysler found itself with a very mature product—the minivan. For a decade or so, the Chrysler minivan was a huge source of income for the company. Then, the market matured, and minivans became more commonplace.

Making the transition from minivans to Sport Utility Vehicles (SUVs) could have been an enormous headache for Chrysler had it not been for the fact that it already had reengineered all of its design and manufacturing processes.

The major gains from driving Internet technologies through every aspect of the automotive business already have been realized. Now, Ford, GM, and DaimlerChrysler must continue to fine tune and tweak the new systems they have in place in order to maintain their positions as industry leaders. I don't see the need for another major architectural change anytime soon. A sensational foundation has been laid, and we can expect to see continued improvements as communication and processor speeds improve over time.

The biggest change I can see in the auto industry, going forward, will be in the relationship companies have with their consumers and dealers. I'm not suggesting that Ford, GM, and DaimlerChrysler ought to move toward a direct-sales model, but there are other areas ripe for improvement. For example, does it really need to be so dastardly difficult to get an appointment to have your car serviced, and why is it so difficult to find out about automotive recall notices?

GM, with its OnStar service, has moved the industry forward in terms of placing communications technology directly into the vehicle. GPS systems will also continue to become cheaper, better integrated, and part of a communications cluster. The challenge for the auto industry and its distribution partners is to take this new technology enablement and turn it into valuable customer interactions. This will require a major new investment in customer-oriented systems.

Today, there is virtually no exploitation of the aftermarket opportunity in the automobile industry, and there is virtually no brand or customer loyalty to Ford, GM, or DaimlerChrysler. Mark my words. Sooner or later, one of these companies is going to achieve that needed breakthrough and start moving hard and fast down that path.

If I were to bet on one of those companies, I'd put my money on GM. I think GM has been thinking about this area of opportunity harder than its competitors.

Also, look forward to seeing more design work being farmed out to parts manufacturers who are becoming bigger and more independent than ever. Today, most of the design work is done internally at Ford, GM, and DaimlerChrysler. After the design work has been completed internally, various parts are put out to bid among the parts manufacturers. In some cases, they know how to design parts better than the in-house design teams at the big three; as a result, parts manufacturers are beginning to contribute toward the overall design of many automotive parts.

A classic example of this can be found in the amount of aluminum that is being used in the industry today. The auto manufacturers that have been so accustomed to designing for steel are not necessarily taking advantage of some of the real benefits of aluminum. However, the parts manufacturers are well aware of these strengths and have been educating the design teams at the big three about its benefits.

Expect to see more and more automotive supply chain partners taking on additional design responsibilities, much like they have done already in the aerospace industry. Also, expect to see marvelous gains in high-speed links and powerful new design tools.

In the April 1934 issue of *Ford News*, automotive pioneer Henry Ford said, "The automobile industry never looked better than it does today."

If only Mr. Ford could see the state of the industry today. That would really set his heart racing, wouldn't it?

CHAPTER 4

Reengineering the Financial Services Industry

Technology weaves its way into our lives in all sorts of interesting ways. When technology was making its way into the financial services world, consumers were watching with millions of skeptical eyes. Consider the case of the world's first Automatic Teller Machines (ATMs).

Nobody knew what an ATM was 35 years ago. More important, very few people thought that machines of any kind could be trusted with their money, but today ATMs are an essential part of the financial services industry.

What was the key to unlocking this new technology? Well, they say that necessity is the mother of invention. A gentleman by the name of Don Wetzel came up with the idea for an ATM while impatiently waiting in line at a Dallas bank back in the 1960s. Together with chief mechanical engineer, Tom Barnes, and electrical engineer, George Chastain, the three men patented the world's first ATM in 1973. There is much debate about *where* the first working ATM was actually installed, but one thing is certain. This was a new technology that was going to take some getting used to.

For example, in the 1970s, when Security Pacific Bank in San Francisco installed its first ATM machine through the walls of its downtown branch, customers standing on the sidewalk outside the bank looked at this new-fangled gizmo, sniffed around a little bit, and then walked away. A marketing challenge was born.

In order to familiarize its customers and *potential customers* with the concept and benefits of an ATM and to warm them up to the idea of actually *using* the machine, Security Pacific Bank hired two smartly dressed, attractive females to ask passersby if they would like to receive a free gift just for trying their new ATM. These folks didn't even have to use their own money to try the new ATM.

All they had to do was punch in any four numbers and out would come a $100 in funny money. Then, they would take their funny money into the branch and receive their choice of either a free toaster or a free coffeemaker, along with a brochure explaining the benefits of ATMs. Those were pretty nice gifts for just punching in four numbers on a machine.

Despite these early demonstrations, a tremendous amount of trepidation existed on the part of consumers, and ATMs took a full three years to really take off. Needless to say, it took a ton of toasters and a carload of coffeemakers to get people to trust the concept of a "teller in a box."

However, trust it they now do, and technology marches on.

4.1 The Financial Services Industry: Ripe for Change

Over the years, technology has played an increasingly important role in the banking industry. However, from its earliest days, government regulation also has played a critical role in shaping the changing nature of this industry.

Beginning in 1916, U.S. commercial banks were prohibited by law from selling insurance. Years later, Congress passed the Banking Act of 1933, which prevented commercial banks from underwriting or brokering securities.

Therefore, it came to be for nearly 50 years that banks stuck to banking, brokerage houses stuck to selling securities, and insurance companies stuck to selling insurance policies.

Then all sorts of market pressures began to impact these industries. Insurance companies began to rely more heavily on investment returns from their reserves as customers migrated to lower cost forms of insurance. Money market funds from brokerage companies began to compete with traditional banking services. All three industries faced significant competition at home and abroad from firms operating without the same set of regulatory constraints. Heavy inflation, emerging technologies, and new sources of competition were causing many financial services institutions to fail and caused others to begin a desperate search for new income streams. In fact, an extraordinary number of bank (1,617) and thrift (1,295) failures occurred in the 1980s and early 1990s, and it was quite clear that sweeping reforms were needed.

The Gramm-Leach-Bliley Financial Services Modernization Act of 1999 finally provided great relief to the U.S. financial services industry. Financial holding companies (FHCs) were now allowed to engage in a myriad of activities, including selling securities, insurance, and banking services. All of a sudden, deregulation changed the value proposition for customers because banks were now allowed to do financial planning, sell insurance, and assist with many other nontraditional services.

The combination of deregulation and Internet technologies made it possible for financial services institutions to integrate a complete portfolio of products and services under a unified umbrella. Some of the most dramatic changes ever to occur in any business category, anywhere in the world, then began.

In light of the U.S. deregulation of its banking industry, the European and Asian financial services communities were removing some of their own restrictions. These financial services companies were finding it difficult to compete internationally, especially after the U.S. financial services industry was deregulated. Therefore, a series of deregulatory moves was made, and the financial services industry, worldwide, began to change and to consolidate.

Interestingly, large numbers of American firms began investing in European and Asian firms, and Asian companies began investing in European and American companies, and, yes, you got it. European companies began investing in Asian and U.S. companies.

Take a look at any number of large U.S. banks today, and you'll discover that they are European owned. It's quite an eye opener.

One example can be found in ABN AMRO, the international banking group, which ranks among the largest in Europe. Years ago, ABN and AMRO used to be separate companies in the Netherlands. Then, they expanded across Europe. Today, they are a single financial services company, and they have done a number of acquisitions in the United States.

These rapid and decisive moves have turned ABN AMRO into one of the top financial services institutions in the world.

A look across the globe yields an amazing sight. Deregulatory efforts since the 1980s have paved the way for "banks without borders" and financial services institutions unimpeded by stifling regulatory requirements. These deregulatory efforts came at a time of rapid technological innovation.

Surely the Internet hastened the rapid changes taking place in the financial services industry. However, like the automotive industry, it was raw commitment, dedicated teamwork, and the vision of executive and IT teams that really helped these changing institutions deliver practical value to their customers.

Of course, Internet technology enabled changes to happen at a brisker pace than they might otherwise have been able to occur. However, none of these changes could have happened in the way they did without the dedication and determination that people in the industry had on delivering enhanced business value to their customers.

A lot of financial services companies have gone belly up during the past couple of decades. Part of the reason for their failures was that these companies didn't clearly articulate their value propositions to their customers. Oftentimes, you can look at the managerial teams at these companies and identify a lack of vision or experience or staying power to deliver on a set of customer value propositions.

4.2 Going Bust and Going Forward

Back in the 1980s and 1990s, all sorts of calamities struck the financial services industry. The collapse of the savings and loan industry was prominently featured, night after night, on the evening news. When the Whitewater scandal erupted, a whole series of speculative real estate deals went bust. All were visible, unsettling, and disheartening.

As a result of these costly failures, the American taxpayers and the Federal Deposit Insurance Corporation (FDIC) got stuck with a huge bailout bill.

Meanwhile, particularly in the United States, the banking industry felt as if it was losing market share to the big investment firms that had more flexibility in terms of the offerings that they were able to put in front of investors. As things like certificates of deposit, money market funds, and a variety of other specialty products began to be offered by these firms, it seemed, to the banking industry, like its territory had been invaded.

Another dimension to the whole U.S. financial services mess was that, particularly in Asia, the integration of financial services was moving faster than it was at home. This situation was causing large companies like Citibank to be unable to offer services domestically that it could offer internationally. It also offered more underlying financial strength for U.S. operations of European and Asian companies.

Frustration ran rampant, and an intense lobbying effort on the part of the U.S. banking and financial services industries began. Their goal was to encourage the government to deregulate the industry, thus putting U.S. companies in a better position to compete on a global scale.

At this time, there was a general feeling among politicos that regulatory schemes, which may have served their purpose decades before, were now stunting industry growth and causing the Federal government to run up enormous regulatory and deposit insurance expenditures.

The time was right for deregulation. Therefore, amid all sorts of financial industry failures, arose a new era, free from many regulatory restrictions and primed for dramatic change.

4.3 A Giant Leap of Faith

After the shackles of regulations had been removed from the hands of the U.S. financial services industry, it became instantly apparent that its success in this brave new world was going to be dependent upon its ability to integrate technology into every aspect of its business.

It was time to think about financial resources in entirely new ways. After all, most money today is held in transfer accounts of some sort. We keep our money in checking accounts, savings accounts, money market funds, and things of that nature. Our money is not held for us in terms of physical piles of cash.

Similarly, if we own U.S. treasury notes, these are no longer silver certificates given to us as proof of ownership. Therefore, the fact of the matter is that there are virtually no physical assets underlying most of our currency these days. We basically own a virtual handful of depository certificates.

It can be an unsettling thought to some, but today we live in a very IT-centric world. Every aspect of today's financial services industry is IT centric.

An insurance company, for example, is basically tracking accounts and taking the premiums you pay and investing them largely in reserves. The interest from the reserves goes into the profit pool of the insurance company and so on and so on.

After that gigantic leap of faith to virtual assets has been made, it's up to the financial services industry to build a rock-solid foundation from which all transactions can be seamlessly performed, tracked, inventoried, and recalled—instantaneously and in a virtual IT environment.

What transpired soon after deregulation was a huge wave of merger activity in the financial services sector. Although today we see fewer firms in this arena, the ones that remain are more integrated than ever before, offering full investment and banking functions.

Visit any large investment firm in the U.S. today, and you can expect to see banklike services offered.

Even with calamitous events such as September 11 or a full-blown economic recession, U.S. financial services companies are generally in much better shape today than they were before deregulation. You can partially credit their success to the IT-driven, effective integration of services in a reasonably responsible and efficient manner.

4.4 Technology's Role in Security Issues

The issue of security is absolutely central when discussing the current state of the financial services industry.

Most banks are preoccupied with physical security. However, at their core, the banking and financial services industries are transactional engines with abundant and unique security issues that go well beyond issues surrounding the physical security of their employees.

The underlying operating principle of any financial services company is that you either want transactions to be completed entirely or to fail completely. Actually, it's a rather complicated process. For any single transaction, a number of accounts have to be debited and credited. That's basic transaction logic. What you don't want is a partially completed transaction. That's when nightmares occur.

Therefore, the financial services industry has made a tremendous financial and strategic investment in transactional integrity. Certainly, this is where IBM's forte has been for many, many years, but other systems and processes are now in place to ensure that kind of transactional integrity. Security is at the very core of those systems. This was relatively difficult to achieve, even when a financial institution used a single, large computer. Understand that today these systems are multilayered and multitiered.

Traditionally, these systems have run on totally independent private networks. In today's world, these transactional systems can be run through an Internet service provider realm using tunneling (a technique used to get data between administrative domains that use a protocol not supported by the Internet) and other advanced technologies. These new technologies are providing a previously unseen level of integrity and security.

In the early 1990s, consumers began to adopt personal financial management software like Quicken. With the advent of the consumer Internet in 1995, financial institutions began to get pressure from customers to download statements directly to these packages. This required banks to use some security mechanism for use on the public Internet.

For the consumer interface to this complexity, it turned out that one of the simplest security solutions was a Secure Sockets Layer (SSL) protocol. This protocol is widely used throughout the financial services industry today. It provides data encryption on all pages and areas where personal data is collected.

How important is security to consumers? One needn't look back much further than New Year's Eve of 1999.

On the eve of the new millennium, fear about the Y2K bug was prevalent around the globe. Earlier in the year, the U.S. Congress had issued a series of reports wherein it expressed its feeling that the financial services industry was really going to be at risk at the stroke of midnight on New Year's Day of 2000. Therefore, toward the end of 1999, people were pulling all their money out of ATMs.

Of course, from the viewpoint of the financial services industry, Y2K was a nonevent. They were, after all, better prepared for the new millennium than any other industry.

It's remarkable. Amid mergers and consolidations, deregulation, the integration of new financial services, the extension of new consumer Internet services, and then the Y2K challenge, the financial services industry came through relatively unscathed.

4.5 The Financial Services Industry Exploits the World's Best Internet Technologies

Looking back over the past several years, it is astonishing to see how well mergers and acquisitions were handled in the financial services industry.

Consider what could be the monumentally difficult task of bringing together two banks or a bank and an investment company. You're going to be faced with two totally separate IT systems and different software products from different vendors. How on earth can these separate worlds be brought together?

I don't think this enormous task would have been feasible without Internet technologies. The Internet enabled financial services companies to integrate their new services closer to the point of use, as opposed to having to integrate all the way to the backend. That let financial services companies deliver an almost immediate set of benefits to their customers. The drumbeat of services never let up, and, as a result, the revenue bases of these newly merged companies continued to expand.

This has generated enough revenue for these companies to go back and fundamentally reengineer their backend systems. Nice.

A good race has also been underway to exploit Internet technologies to reach out to branch offices. Today, you have an ATM link. You also have the powerful office productivity linkages. In addition, a great deal of work is happening in the area of harmonizing and integrating the various information networks being used by branch offices. Better security messages are also being developed every day.

The need to integrate because of mergers and acquisitions, the need to harmonize communications activities, and the need to bring services to market all drove an unprecedented wave of investment in Internet technologies by the financial services industry.

IBM's growth from 1995 through the present day has been largely based on its gross revenues emanating from sales to the financial services industry. It happens to be the largest industry that IBM serves. Cisco Systems also can attribute its massive growth during the past five or six years to the work it has done in this industry.

The auto industry was the prime driver of Internet technology through the mid 1990s. From that point forward, the financial services and banking industries have been the prime drivers of this new technology.

4.6 Giving Credit Where Credit Is Due

Wiring the financial services industry also meant making it a more secure world for the likes of Visa and MasterCard and American Express, to name a few credit card companies. There was quite the battle among the big players in this area about which technology protocol ought to be used to secure credit card transactions.

Certain Internet hobbyists wanted to have a hand in this debate. They thought that, with the new wave of Internet technologies, credit card transactions could be dramatically improved. The problem with the hobbyists' suggestions was that such schemes would have significantly slowed down the implementation of new services while dramatically adding to the cost of credit card transactions, and at the same time providing very little in the way of increased security.

A middle ground was needed.

Prior to the Internet, people used to take their credit cards into a merchant where all sorts of possibilities for fraud existed. The merchant would keep a carbon copy of the transaction. An employee of the merchant also could keep a carbon copy of the transaction or just write the credit card information down on a separate piece of paper. If you decided to purchase something over the telephone, you would be dependent upon the integrity and supervision of the person with whom you left your credit card number.

Next, there was a major problem with repudiation. Someone would buy something using a credit card, only later to insist that no such item was ever purchased. "Hey, it must have been somebody else using my credit card!" they would say.

Surprisingly, when these credit card transactions moved to the Internet, it became more difficult to steal credit card numbers. In fact, Internet transactions have had a reasonably good record of success, oftentimes eclipsing the records of telephone transactions or merchant transactions. This success has encouraged more folks to buy products and services over the Internet, accounting for almost 2 percent of all purchases in the United States. It's not a huge percentage, but it is a big number, and it's growing.

It's wonderful to see that credit card companies like Visa, MasterCard, and American Express are all guaranteeing the integrity of Internet transactions, just as they do with transactions in the physical universe.

The most likely scenario for Internet fraud is not found when credit card numbers are stolen during a transaction. It occurs most often when servers are hacked, and that happens very infrequently.

Therefore, all in all, credit must be given to the credit card companies. They clearly understood their role in the physical universe as guarantors of transactional integrity and successfully translated that model to the electronic world. They've learned to exploit the Internet to great advantage—for themselves and for their customers.

4.7 Cloudy Skies for the Insurance Industry

The challenges in the insurance industry were and are quite different from those in the banking and financial services industries.

The vision that people had going into the 1990s was to create one-stop shops wherein a customer could buy insurance, take care of any banking needs, and tap into a variety of financial services. However, a funny thing happened on the way to this vision.

First of all, the insurance industry trailed significantly behind the technological progress being made by the banking and financial services industries. Second, a number of catastrophic losses were endured during this time by the insurance industry, most notably due to hurricanes, floods, and other natural disasters. Finally, the insurance industry suffered from its long-term dependence on somewhat speculative investments, some of which went bust. Throughout the 1990s, these forces collectively contributed to a very unfavorable economic climate for the U.S. insurance industry and an almost total meltdown of the medical insurance industry.

Whereas the banking and financial services industries were on the cutting edge of the adoption of new Internet technologies, the insurance industry was on the complete opposite side of the spectrum. Insurance companies were the laggards in this technology revolution, and they were going to pay a price.

Further, the insurance industry continued to agonize over sales and distribution-channel issues. In financial services, the likes of Schwab and Ameritrade fundamentally upset the models of the industry, and others were required to follow suit. There has not been a major disruptive competitor in the insurance industry.

Not all insurance companies failed to hop on board the technology express. Take for example the United States Automobile Association (USAA).

4.8 A Salute to USAA

One of the most technologically advanced insurance companies in the world is USAA, which has served the U.S. military community and its families since the 1920s. I've been a USAA member ever since I went to Air Force Officer Training School in 1973.

Traditionally, USAA had as its primary insurance customers military officers, who had great difficulty getting insurance because they moved around so much. When the U.S. military downsized, USAA decided to broaden its customer base to include not only military officers, but also the entire military and anyone who previously had been a member of the U.S. military.

There is a funny thing about the insurance industry. A lot of insurance companies didn't understand the difference between officers and enlisted men and women. They viewed enlisted folks as a bunch of drunken boozers and officers as a bunch of financially struggling folks and frankly weren't much interested in insuring either group. None of them understood the unique problems associated with frequent reassignments and temporary deployments. Therefore, a group of military officers basically decided to form their own insurance company and insure their own people.

Today, USAA is one of the largest insurance companies in the world, and it certainly is among the most financially healthy. You may be surprised to know that USAA is also the most technologically intensive of the U.S. insurance companies. This was important as USAA took full advantage of deregulatory legislation by expanding into the broad scope of financial services.

USAA is well known throughout the insurance and financial services industries and is often cited as a sterling example among insurance companies. In addition, USAA is huge these days. It's a member-owned Fortune 500 company that owns and manages more than $60 billion in assets. It has 4.6 million members and is growing. Today, it serves active duty personnel, National Guard and Reserve enlisted personnel, officers and officer candidates, and their families.

There's a joke among those folks who have made their careers in the military. It's that the best veterans' benefit that you'll ever get is becoming a member of USAA. Do you know what? I tend to agree with them!

Therefore, here we have a shining example of a financial services company that has wired itself from end to end. How did this come to pass?

One thing that made it so easy for USAA to become so technologically savvy is that it was unencumbered by a traditional agent network. USAA has a completely centralized approach to how it handles member services. This has been important, especially when you realize that USAA members are found throughout the world.

USAA's customers are a very mobile lot, and USAA has to contend with the challenge of Temporary Duty (TDY). When its members go on a 6-month TDY or a 30-day TDY, they still need all of the traditional financial services to accompany them. This truly did force USAA to centralize its customer service function and to focus on automation.

Through my work at both IBM and HP, I had some involvement with State Farm. Unlike USAA, State Farm has had to contend with thousands of semi-independent agents. It has been quite the challenge to provide a coherent IT environment to State Farm agents, not to mention the dilemma State Farm has had in supporting that environment. Also, through the years, the agents at State Farm have found an uncomfortable financial burden placed upon them to invest in technology.

Integration issues were enormous at State Farm as well. The IT costs of delivering on a distributed network have been huge. This has caused State Farm to spend more of its IT budget just solving these types of problems, rather than spending its IT dollars on backend integration like USAA has been able to do.

Therefore, while USAA has been able to integrate its services on behalf of its customers, other insurance companies have been spending huge portions of their IT budgets on issues that USAA does not have to address.

Nevertheless, USAA has been slow to exploit Internet technologies throughout its business processes. One can safely predict that this will be one of USAA's top priorities as we move forward in the 21st century.

Meanwhile, USAA has become much more financially stable and disciplined than other insurance companies. That has provided it with a nice launching pad from which to get into the financial services and banking arenas.

The winning strategy at USAA has been to understand its customers' needs and to evolve a portfolio of services that turns the company into a one-stop shop, with a very seamless and powerful customer interface.

USAA has done a beautiful job of reengineering itself to better serve its customers, and Fidelity is not far behind in this technology hit parade.

4.9 High Fidelity

Fidelity has done an incredible job of linking its services out to the Web, thus making it accessible through its agents. This has helped Fidelity maintain its high market share and its admirable status within the financial services industry.

Today, Fidelity serves more than 17 million customers and manages over $900 billion in assets.

Some of the honors Fidelity received in 2001 were the following:

- #1 in customer satisfaction among online brokerage houses – J.D. Power and Associates
- #1 online brokerage for mainstream investors—*MONEY* magazine
- #1 ranking for one-stop shoppers—Gomez
- Best of the Web—*Forbes* magazine

Fidelity has been particularly adept at setting up regional service centers. This has given Fidelity's customers easy access to their accounts, not only through the Web, but also through their regional service representatives.

Fidelity has done a much better job than most financial institutions of making its services Internet accessible. Take a look at Fidelity's Web site (www.fidelity.com) and you'll see what I mean.

Fidelity has been around since 1946. A combination of hard work, outstanding leadership, and innovative technologies has helped Fidelity grow, change, and prosper through the years.

Fidelity was perhaps the first large financial services company to recognize that all of its products are essentially IT-created products. The Fidelity IT team pioneered the development of new financial services offerings through rapid system deployment methodologies. The Fidelity team then used the power of the Internet to link these products and the IT systems supporting them into a coherent and powerful set of offerings for individual and institutional customers. It also has allowed Fidelity offerings to be well integrated into the human resource systems of the companies for which it provides services.

Fidelity serves as an excellent case study for those working in the financial services arena.

4.10 Banking on the Future

In the years ahead, I expect to see another round of integration within the financial services industry.

Look closely at the offerings of most players in this industry, and you'll see products that look like they were bolted together after the fact. This is partly due to some of the early indigestion problems experienced within this industry, as it has attempted to wire itself for the future. Although companies have pulled together fairly well, their mutual IT products still need some refinement and reengineering.

The problem that a lot of us have today is that it's still somewhat complicated to manage our funds, and move them from one account to another. There just aren't a lot of intuitive, automated tools to help us.

My opinion is that the most progressive financial services companies will move toward a model wherein their customers have preference profiles. These profiles will make it easier for financial institutions to customize offerings for individuals based upon the preferences that they have previously expressed.

Therefore, for example, based upon your preference for allowable risk ratios, your financial institution could use advanced Internet technologies to suggest the perfect blend of equities, money market funds, and cash accounts to meet your requirements.

These enhancements to the customer experience will require another major round of investment in the IT infrastructure of the financial services industry.

As far as the insurance industry is concerned, it will have to join the 21st century. This is an industry that can be characterized by an overwhelming amount of manual labor. Its processes are still very archaic, and the backend IT systems that the insurance industry has deployed don't touch their customers in any meaningful way.

From the sale of the insurance policy through the delivery of the policy itself, very little automation takes place and, typically, is only in islands when it does.

I think it's going to take a company like Ameritrade or e-Schwab to disrupt the insurance industry. There just hasn't been a standout pioneer in the insurance industry capable of causing a major shift. However, mark my words. This industry is due for a shakeup.

All it will take will be a single company with a relentless vision of what it *could* become to so disrupt the foundations of the industry that all companies will be forced to move in the same bold direction.

For many years, behind the scenes, the Citibanks of the world have been working on consolidation with the same kind of passion with which Ford approached its vertical integration and quality problems and with which Chrysler approached its design problems.

While Schwab was working on its particular design problems, Fidelity was working on its own problems. Meanwhile, Citigroup and a variety of other large banking firms were working on their own vertical integration problems. Massive reengineering occurred, and each of these companies found itself once again on the fast track to profit.

If you look at financial services firms today, you'll notice that their commission rates have fallen dramatically, and not all of these firms are equally profitable. However, some of them have figured out how to be reasonably profitable on much thinner margins. They've done this by driving incredible efficiencies throughout every sector of their business.

Success in the financial services industry is also going to depend on the ability of individual companies to develop more valuable relationships with their customers—relationships that develop more quickly, last longer, and remain increasingly profitable.

This will be a customer-centered revolution, which will feature greater depths in product and service offerings. Any way that you look at it, we are likely to cash in on the benefits of this new wave of customer services.

And speaking of cashing in…

Even the relatively simple technology in today's ATMs is providing a level of security of which few folks are aware. An acquaintance of mine who is a retired vice president for Security Pacific Bank tells me the amusing story of middle-age adults who occasionally come into the bank complaining that their bank statements indicate ATM withdrawals that they swear they didn't make. After a bit of research, bank personnel can match ATM withdrawal dates and times on these accounts to the photographs taken automatically by ATMs for each transaction. Amazing how often the crooks in these photos end up being the teenage kids of these middle-age folks—teens who apparently knew their parents' pin numbers and "borrowed" their credit cards.

Good ol' technology! Sometimes, you just can't beat it!

CHAPTER 5

Reengineering the Travel Industry

Amid long lines at airline counters, embarrassing strip searches at security gates, and lost luggage at our ultimate destinations, it's easy to forget that, when we travel, we are tapping into one of the most remarkable service industries on the planet.

However, service has been at the very core of the airline industry since its earliest days. In the 1920s, before passenger service was envisioned, Walter T. Varney began the first commercial flights in this country, bringing U.S. mail from Point A to Point B. The quarters were cramped and noisy, and, after the sacks of mail were put on board, very little room was left for the pilot or the crew. Adding to the airsickness quotient was the fact that there was no heating in the winter or air conditioning in summer. Nevertheless, the mail was getting delivered, and creature comforts were on their way.

Businessmen were eyeing these early flights and wondering if groups of travel-hungry passengers could be transported just as easily as sacks of mail. As larger airplanes were being built during the 1930s, the answer became quite clear to them. They recognized that passengers, unlike those sacks of mail, could be turned into valuable *repeat* customers if they were treated to special comforts and extravagances while airborne.

The problem, as United Airlines saw it, was how to encourage customers to use their services when America was in the grips of its deepest economic depression. Their solution was clever. United knew that many young, female nurses were without jobs at that time, and they decided that "sky girls," as they would become known, could become great public relations (PR) vehicles for the company. The word was out on the street that United was looking for its first sky girls, and only registered nurses need apply.

When the Boeing 247 joined United Airline's fleet in 1933, the new nurses/stewardesses began serving all 10 passengers on board these early commercial flights. In those days, a simple flight from New York to Chicago would last five hours, which was long by today's standards, but lightning quick in those days.

The first coast-to-coast flights on the Boeing 247s took just 21 hours. Of course, the cabins weren't pressurized in those days, and planes flying on these journeys had to stop several times to refuel. However, the passengers were served hot meals and drinks, making these flights considerably easier to tolerate.

By 1936, up to 21 passengers could fly on the new DC-3 twin-engine planes, and, in a mere 18 hours, they could travel from coast to coast. Some of these DC-3s were even converted to luxurious sleeper planes. Imagine how exquisite the experience of flying in one of these planes was. After a relaxing nap in your private berth, you would be served extravagant meals at beautiful, linen-covered tables, featuring lovely china and sterling silver.

That sure beats today's plastic tray tables, paper cups, and salted peanuts.

Trans World Airlines (TWA) and Pan Am developed similar breakthrough service to Europe and Asia using the Lockheed Super Constellation and Boeing Stratocruiser. It's hard to believe today, but, in the 1950s, most travelers to Europe and Asia went by boat, and trips to parts of Asia took as long as three months each way.

It was a different world back then.

However, what the travel industry may have lost in terms of sheer elegance and pampered service, it has gained in terms of professionalism, speed, scalability, safety, reach, and profitability. What was then an art is a science today.

5.1 The World Shrinks Before Our Very Eyes

Modern jet travel has allowed the world to shrink before our very eyes. Virtually no region of the world is unreachable anymore. Where once you only could experience the world through folklore or books, today you can hop on a plane and visit nearly any spot on the globe in a matter of hours.

It was evident from the earliest days of passenger air travel that eventually some sort of communications system would have to be developed so that airlines could cooperate with one another.

Such a system was developed in 1949, when Integrated Telecommunications and Information Solutions (SITA) was founded by seven airlines, each eager to take advantage of cost and communications efficiencies. Based in Paris, SITA included:

• Air France
• Royal Dutch Airlines (KLM)
• Sabena
• TWA
• British European Airways Corporation (BEAC) and British Overseas Airways Corporation
• Wedish A.G Aerotransport, Danish Det Danske Luftfartselskab A/S, and Norwegian Det Norske Luftfartselskap
• Swissair

SITA evolved because the airlines realized that they needed to establish communication connections among all of the air terminals around the world, and that it was far too inefficient to have all of the world's airlines build their own networks into every terminal.

As its global membership roster grew, SITA built a common network infrastructure that linked the entire worldwide travel industry. By the mid-1950s, SITA was transmitting more than 12 million messages throughout its network each year. It also provided the check-in equipment for all of the airlines.

This equipment allowed airlines to switch gates or switch check-in counters automatically. An elaborate infrastructure allowed them to do this quickly and efficiently. The beauty of SITA was that all of the major airlines of the world were shareholders in this company and benefited equally from the services it provided.

Not only were airline terminals connected by means of this powerful global network, individual airlines were also able to use the system to cross-connect to various other airlines.

By the 1960s, SITA was using computers to exchange data throughout the aviation world. This new technology was a boon to the industry, and, by the 1970s, SITA was handling almost 300 million messages each year. A decade later, SITA was handling more than 30 billion messages each year. Today, SITA has nearly 700 members and is the world's largest provider of integrated telecommunications and information solutions to the air transportation industry.

Now that is an impressive accomplishment.

5.2 Reservations about Reservations

In the early days of U.S. commercial aviation, the Federal Aviation Administration (FAA) basically coordinated the air route system in the United States, and it closely regulated which routes the carriers could serve. However, deregulatory measures eased those early restrictions, and, today, the U.S. airline industry is built upon a hub-and-spoke system.

It was pretty common practice before the hub-and-spoke system was put into place that you would have to deal with more than one airline carrier unless you were flying on nonstop flights between major cities, such as New York and Los Angeles. Therefore, there was a great urgency among the U.S. airlines to invest in networking capabilities and to collaborate with one another on a minute-by-minute basis.

Thus arose in the 1960s a network of highly sophisticated airline reservation systems in the United States, among which Semi-Automated Business Reservations Environment (SABRE) was the most notable. Owned by AMR, Inc., the parent company of American Airlines, SABRE was developed to provide travel agents with the ability to book trips directly with the airlines. When the first system went online in 1964, it resulted in an immediate staff savings of 30 percent and an error rate of less than 1 percent. It also gave American Airlines a competitive advantage that lasted seven years. In 1976, the first SABRE terminal was installed in a travel agent's office, and by year-end, 130 of the largest agents were online. Eighty-six percent of them used SABRE.

This was a masterstroke on the part of American Airlines.

All of a sudden, American had a way to reach out to travel agents. With the help of SITA, American Airlines built a network that could extend to every travel agent in the country, and that began the race to put computer terminals in travel agents' offices everywhere. Overnight, it was no longer necessary for customers to call the airlines to book their travel. They felt that travel agents lived to serve them, and, in a way, they did.

This breakthrough success caused a few early challenges from government regulators. When travel agents typed in the desired departure and arrival cities, American Airlines programmed the network to bring up *its* flights first. An antitrust suit was filed, and American Airlines wisely made a management decision that SABRE would be set up as an independent subsidiary that would not automatically favor American Airlines flights over others. By 1988, the SABRE system stored 31 million airfares that could be combined to create more than 1 billion fare options. During fare price wars, up to 45 million fare changes a day could occur. Staggering, isn't it?

Interestingly, the bulk of American Airlines' profits these days come not from its flights, but from its SABRE system. It's really an amazing success story.

American Airlines truly stands out as a good corporate citizen, too. Its management team genuinely saw the potential of making the SABRE system truly objective, and this ultimately made the business potential for the SABRE system that much greater.

Other reservations systems are out there today, including the CoVia system and the Galileo system, but SABRE owns the lion's share of the business.

SABRE earns a transaction fee on every airline ticket booked through its system. In doing so, SABRE has become one of the largest IT companies in the world. It's just amazing to consider the amount of computing and networking power in that system.

In the early days of the SABRE system, travel agents were earning a 7 percent commission on the travel itineraries they booked. The entry barriers into this business were very low for travel agents, and people were getting into this business in droves. They'd basically get a little training, put a terminal in place, which carried one of these reservations systems, and, voilà, they were in business.

Thus, during this era, there was an explosion of little Mom-and-Pop travel agencies. They were popping up everywhere. Every strip mall in America seemed to have one or two of these little travel boutiques.

Interestingly, a large percentage of these agents were doing this work "on the side." They did very little booking for customers, but lots of booking for *personal* travel, for which they received considerable discounts, not only for themselves, but also for their families and friends.

It was a strange sight to behold, and it was all caused by the fact that American Airlines had a major technology breakthrough when it developed its SABRE operation. American had found a way to extend technology into the hands of travel agents, causing a complete paradigm shift from the way airline tickets used to be purchased.

5.3 Putting the Brakes on the Commission Gravy Train

One interesting development regarding the reengineering of the travel industry arose from the fact that the industry had built up quite an elaborate IT infrastructure, well before the Internet came along. This allowed the travel industry to move fairly rapidly into some of the newest areas of technology when the Internet revolution arrived.

Back in the 1990s, as the Internet started to get hot, the SABRE folks were eyeing this new technology with eager anticipation. SABRE, of course, was the number one reservations system out there, and they already were technologically sophisticated, especially about networks. They also already had in place a huge engine that was driving the bulk of the world's airline transactions.

Then SABRE, sensing a tremendous opportunity, started a new Web-based operation called Travelocity. It was a brilliant concept. Whereas previously it was laborious for consumers to use the travel agent system to book travel itineraries, the folks working on Travelocity bolted on a fairly user-friendly frontend to the system. While taking advantage of the technology infrastructure they already had in place, the SABRE team was able to go to market with Travelocity in very short order.

To some extent, I think SABRE was able to forestall some of the airlines from moving into this new space because online booking was available so early from the industry leader in reservations. SABRE had a great brand name, and, of course, Travelocity caught the attention of consumers in a big way, right out of the gate.

However, customer service issues would loom large for this emerging Web-based service. For one thing, customers had to give a travel agent's name, so that the travel agent could get a ticket out to the customer. Sensing an opportunity, clever engineers at Travelocity were working hard, behind the scenes, on an e-ticket paradigm.

The drive behind all of these electronic efforts was the desire to take some of the costs out of ticketing. At this stage, airlines were paying a 7 percent commission to travel agents. The cost of printing a ticket was running somewhere between $10 and $20.

With the onset of the e-ticketing revolution, airlines could go directly to customers, and the industry cost for travel agents basically fell to about half of what it was before.

The exploitation of Internet technologies has allowed major costs to be taken out of the industry, and the savings passed along to consumers. To a large extent, that explains a lot of the growth that has gone on in the travel industry since 1995.

Even with the tragic events of September 11, the travel industry is much larger today than it was back in 1995. It has experienced astronomical growth. A lot of people attribute that to the .com revolution. I think that's partially correct. However, also playing a huge role in the growth of the travel industry has been the fact that travel has become an increasingly better value to consumers. This has certainly boosted the amount of recreational travel that people are doing nowadays.

In light of the events on September 11, many analysts felt that airline travel might take years to bounce back to pre-September 11 levels. Travel has slowly bounced back, though not to pre-September 11 levels, and the forecast for this industry is once again improving.

The picture is not as rosy for Delta Airlines, which announced on March 14, 2002, that it would no longer pay base commissions on tickets sold in the United States and Canada. Delta posted a net loss of $1.2 billion in 2001. As Delta announced this move, most industry analysts expected competitors to follow suit, and, in the subsequent two weeks, most other carriers did.

Nevertheless, from a macroeconomics point of view, the drive for efficiency in the airline industry has saved the industry and allowed it to survive and eventually to prosper, even during its most challenging times.

5.4 An Expedient Twist in the Game

Investments in technology have worked wonders for the travel industry. Of course, technology-driven market leaders in any industry will always be challenged for their coveted positions. Thus came the Microsoft Network (MSN) with Expedia, its entry into the travel industry.

Consider the market indicators. From 1995 to 2000, there was a major consolidation of the travel agency landscape. A lot of the original Mom-and-Pop shops were being driven out of business or had to affiliate themselves with larger travel companies. Efficiency was being driven into every segment of the industry.

Meanwhile, Microsoft was building upon its enormous online presence throughout the world. Microsoft was able to touch consumers on any number of online levels, and its brand equity was about to carry it with lightning speed into the online travel industry.

Microsoft was able to introduce and build its Expedia property more rapidly than most thought possible. The way Microsoft did this was to construct Expedia very much like a traditional travel agent, only with a user interface that spelled fun.

Take a look at www.expedia.com. You'll quickly see why Expedia has become one of the most profitable features of the MSN operation.

You can almost hear the shockwaves that ran through the travel industry when the MSN introduced Expedia. All of a sudden, you had a company like Microsoft, with all of its reach, coming into the travel industry and presenting the possibility that it would be able to replace systems like Travelocity and the SABRE airline system. Some even worried that Microsoft would be able to replace the airlines and their customer loyalty programs to a large extent.

The market entry by Microsoft was viewed as a severe competitive threat. I think this was one of the reasons for the continued legal pressure being placed on Microsoft for having operated as a monopoly. After all, it is generally illegal to use your monopoly status to extend your monopoly into other areas. Yet, that appears to be what Microsoft has tried to do in a number of areas, including banking and finance and the travel industry.

With regard to Expedia, the battleground is really drawn around the issue of bundling online service icons on the desktop and the bundling of the Microsoft Windows Explorer into the operating system. Despite the fact that Netscape has essentially disappeared, when it once had the industry leadership position, the Justice Department has pretty much rolled over and played dead. It will be interesting to watch the course of the America Online (AOL)—as the acquirer of Netscape—antitrust lawsuit against Microsoft. However, Microsoft's woes are far from over, even if it gets through the current round of antitrust problems. It's likely that Microsoft will find itself fenced in, in terms of the opportunities to use its current monopoly to extend into other areas, such as the travel industry.

One thing is certain. The conduct remedies that Microsoft has agreed to in the past don't work. Microsoft agrees to change its conduct, and then it just doesn't change. Time will tell if Microsoft can continue to dodge legal bullets.

Nevertheless, the current legal environment in which Microsoft finds itself is likely to chill the company enough to avoid expanding too aggressively going forward. It appears as if its market share in the travel industry has stabilized. Therefore, I don't see any great move on the part of Microsoft to rock the travel industry boat any further, at least until stiller waters prevail.

5.5 The Irresistible Allure of Perks

The advent of the Internet also allowed airlines to develop their own direct booking sites. Because they no longer had to build a private network to reach customers, the cost of adding additional servers to their current reservation system to do the direct customer interface was quite low. Airlines drew customers to these sites with new services, including updates on flight status and a frequent-flyer mileage bonus for booking online. They also experimented with last-minute specials and direct email communications with customers.

The airlines' sites have suffered from some chronic problems, however. First, the sites tended to quote higher fares to customers than could be obtained through the other reservation systems. Despite many complaints, most airline Web sites still do not quote the best fares. Second, many of the sites look like customer interfaces were bolted on. It can be difficult to navigate the menus and systems, and some of the parts (like the frequent-flyer statements) are obviously simple Hypertext Markup Language (HTML) versions of the previously printed reports.

Today, a number of airlines have reached out to touch their customers directly. The airlines have used their frequent-flyer programs to increase customer loyalty, and it seems to be working.

On top of this most valued perk, the airlines are adding more and more customer services. For example, even if you have booked your travel through a travel agent, you'll be able to go online and see your itinerary at your host airline's Web site. You can also request upgrades more easily online.

All of the airlines are pushing hard to get electronic statements to their customers. They've done this not only in a reaction to the enormous economic strain they've been under since September 11, but also in response to the anthrax scare in the U.S. Postal Service. Each of these pressures has accelerated the airlines' move toward electronic statements. Coincidentally, that has contributed further to the woes of the U.S. Postal Service because it is about to lose yet another source of First Class mail, which is its most profitable revenue source.

The practice of offering perks to customers took off like a rocket as deregulation and automation hit the airline industry. With the new hub-and-spoke system in place, airlines rushed to hold on to their customers' loyalty. The airlines landed upon a powerful formula for retaining their frequent flyers, building programs that encouraged customer loyalty by offering perks heretofore unknown by all but the most elite of airline passengers.

For some time, there was a battle between corporate travel departments and individual travelers over who was the rightful owner of these new frequent-flyer miles. The airlines have consistently insisted that the miles belong to the flyers, not the corporations paying for their business travel. The corporations have argued that they are the rightful owners of the miles because it is their money that earned the miles. The airlines have been pretty darn successful in winning this battle over the miles, much to the delight of the millions of exhausted road warriors working around the world today.

It is now easier for corporate travel departments to ensure compliance with corporate travel policies and still allow individual travelers the preference of giving loyalty back to the airlines. As long as the flights chosen by these travelers fall within an acceptable price range, corporate travelers are often allowed to choose to fly their preferred airlines. Internet technology has made the reconciliation between preferred airlines and preferred fares a snap for corporate travel departments.

It appears as if we've reached a fairly stable point in terms of the debate and discussion that has raged around frequent-flyer programs and who owns the miles. However, interestingly, these frequent-flyer benefits may be taxed sometime in the future.

On another front, we are seeing an interesting twist on the airport security measures currently being undertaken. The airlines are asking for their most cherished frequent travelers to be released from the hassles other passengers face at airport security stations. The airlines are suggesting that they know their best customers intimately and that, if these customers offered just a bit more information about themselves, they should be rewarded with unimpeded passage through airport security. The airlines suggest that this would not only be good for its best customers, but it would also be an excellent way to alleviate some of the congestion at security checkpoints. They already are offering expedited security services at some major hubs.

5.6 Increasing Profitability in the Travel Industry

The exploitation of Internet technologies has allowed the travel industry to reduce its transaction costs by more than 50 percent. Although fuel and labor costs are typically the largest financial drains on the airlines, a significant cost savings can still be gained with regard to transaction costs. After all, this industry is huge, and, with millions and millions of transactions occurring at all times, great benefits can be gained by reducing costs in this area.

I guarantee that the industry would not have been able to decrease its transaction costs during the past five years in the dramatic fashion it did were it not for the Internet. You can directly attribute these savings of 50 percent and more to the Internet.

Not only have we seen a reduction in the number of travel agencies, we've also seen a reduction in the cost of printing tickets, which was all made possible by the e-ticketing phenomenon. Save money, save trees. Everyone wins.

When SITA originally built its network, it did so around international industry standards, not some vendor's proprietary communications architecture. Any number of vendors would have loved to have the SITA network built on their propriety architectures. However, SITA wisely selected the X.25 protocol, and that ultimately gave it the independence and the ability to migrate much faster to the Internet when that time came. Believe me, many other industries have gone down the path of proprietary vendor communications protocols, and they have ended up paying dearly for their mistakes.

The airlines have adopted the Internet pervasively throughout their operations. They have connected their own sites to CoVia, Galileo, SABRE, and SITA. If you're an airline in business anywhere on Earth, and you have to connect to a worldwide airport terminal facility, you are going to have to touch the SITA network in some fashion.

The SITA network ranges from Jakarta to Paris to Atlanta. Atlanta is one of the largest hubs in the SITA network, by the way. SITA has one of the world's largest networks running nonproprietary protocols.

By the time the airline industry brought Internet protocols into its communications network in the mid-1990s, these technologies had already proven to be extremely effective in the auto industry. The auto industry drove reliability into the very core of Internet technologies. Along with the work done at academic institutions, these two powerhouses were the real pioneers of the Internet. They relied upon the Internet on a day-to-day basis for achieving their core missions.

In academia, in particular, research missions were—and are—driven very heavily by collaborations over the Internet, which have made the Internet mission critical among those working in institutions of higher education.

Then, in the mid to late 1980s, the auto industry grabbed the Internet baton and ran with it full speed. By the time the airline industry got around to adopting the technology, it was well proven and ready to roll.

Again, I'd like to stress that airline people probably had more experience in deploying reliable vendor-independent networks than anyone else. They already employed a solid collection of first-class network engineers, who took to Internet technology like ducks take to water.

Because they had originally built most of their systems around nonproprietary communication protocols, the migration to the Internet was relatively easy. By the way, the European Research Network also had been running the X.25 protocol, and they also had made the easy transition to Internet technology at about the same time as the U.S. airline industry.

A series of tremendously fortunate choices was made over a long period of time, and a seasoned and knowledgeable team was in place when the time came to deploy Internet technologies professionally throughout the industry. The reliability of this new technology was never a question, but the scalability of the servers was.

Why was this important? Well, during the late 1980s, especially during fare wars, the SABRE system was sometimes handling 45 million fare changes a day. The sheer volume of hits running through the SABRE system was, and *is,* incredible.

In 1986, SABRE installed the first automated yield management system. This system allowed the airlines to know, at any given moment, how many seats remained unsold on any given flight. Seats on airplanes are very perishable, you know. If a plane takes off with an empty seat, the airline can never recoup that revenue, so airlines have used very sophisticated algorithms to price seats in order to fill them.

Typically, airlines sell a lot of seats a long time before the flight takes off, and these seats sell for very low fares. However, the airlines don't want to sell more seats than they have to at those low fares because they can sell higher-priced seats closer to the actual date of travel, usually to business travelers. Therefore, an art has developed in not overselling low fares so much that you miss the chance for last-minute profit taking.

The airlines have long maintained the stance that casual travelers are the ones having the most flexibility. By using the casual travelers to fill up their planes, these passengers are actually subsidizing the business travelers. Of course, business travelers often have a totally different opinion of who is subsidizing whom.

At any rate, the yield management systems used by the airlines were pretty sophisticated from the very beginning, and, after the hub-and-spoke systems were put in place, profit management skills moved to new heights.

The ability to get pricing information from independent services or semi-independent services has really allowed the airlines to do a better job of targeting their fares. Most people have no idea of the vast amount of complex transaction work that goes on behind the scenes in just the day-to-day operation of the airlines in terms of their pricing and the management of their routing.

On any flight you might take, you can expect that folks traveling on your airplane might have paid 20 or 30 different fares for a seat just like yours. Some may have purchased their tickets from ticket consolidators who bought big blocks of cheap tickets. Some may have purchased their tickets that day, meaning you are likely to have received a better fare. Some may be traveling for free, taking advantage of their frequent-flyer miles.

In any case, just keep in mind that an airline seat is a perishable commodity. If the seat remains empty, the airlines can never again get revenue out of it for that particular flight in which it remained empty.

This situation obviously has created an incredibly intense transactional environment that sits behind the scenes, away from the view of customers. There is a big race now among the major airlines, the SABRE organization, CoVia, and others to make their seats available on the Internet. What this means is that a huge transactional backend will now have a frontend bolted onto it. Originally, the airlines bolted on a Sun Systems frontend, but quickly discovered scalability and reliability problems.

It's been a scalability horse race on the UNIX environment since 1995, and, out of this race, has come thoroughbreds like HP's Superdome system.

It wasn't so much that the Internet wasn't ready for the airline industry. It was that the massive amounts of data being driven through the systems required five or six layers of technology working simultaneously and harmoniously for each of the millions of transactions being created each day.

It takes a very complex application and service delivery architecture to network the airline industry seamlessly. This is the foundation on which HP has built its Utility Data Center.

One of the problems that a lot of businesses have had in driving the Internet through their business processes is that, traditionally, it has taken a lot of very skilled people to assist with these efforts. One of our big customers at HP recently joked that it sure would be nice if the next time his company deploys an application, he didn't have to hire two Ph.D.s from a database company, two Ph.D.s from a server company, two Ph.D.s from a storage company, and two Ph.D.s from an application company.

Now, mind you, I have nothing against Ph.D.s. I am one, after all. For heaven's sake, though, it shouldn't take a truckload of us to deploy a new application.

Luckily, because of the Web, it has become so much easier to deploy new applications. The trick now becomes making sure that your new communications and applications delivery infrastructure is maintainable and scaleable.

Some companies have the talent internally to make sure that these new systems are maintained and scaled properly. The airlines and the auto industry are quite adept at this. This has given them first-mover advantages.

Other industries, like the insurance industry, have really struggled with this. Unlike the airline and automotive industries, the insurance industry simply lacks a scientific and technical core and the willingness to interact directly with their customers.

Professional services organizations have certainly been able to assist the slow movers. One of the reasons IBM sponsored the Olympics was to perfect its scalability formula. In both the Atlanta and Nagano Olympics, IBM was able to get very good at highly scaleable deployments. Of course, IBM never really cracked the labor problem, and, because its systems weren't as automated as they might have been, a whole lot of Ph.D.s were still needed during the deployment.

The approach at HP has been quite different. We tend to be more of a product company. We certainly have a highly capable professional services organization, but our strong suit has really been in the area of creating new products.

That's why HP has moved much more decisively toward building a Utility Data Center. We've been working very hard to define the various architectures regarding how people deploy new Internet-based communications systems and, as a result, have developed a fairly sophisticated networking fabric into our Utility Data Center. This will allow previously labor-intensive work to be automated, and the more automated these systems become means the more accelerated one's journey becomes on the fast track to profit.

5.7 Up, Up, and Away!

Looking forward in the travel industry, I'm certain that there will be increasing pressure for better customer identification. Although this is a very sensitive area involving privacy issues, the airlines are likely to push for additional conveniences for their frequent flyers, especially when it comes to check-in and security gate procedures. They view this not only as a benefit for their best customers, but also as a benefit for infrequent flyers, who will enjoy a security system that is less overburdened at various security checkpoints.

This also would be an effective way to reduce overall security costs while improving the overall experience of the traveling public. I expect there to be a lot of debate about this topic. I also expect the airline industry to be an early adopter of biometric technology, which it will likely use to identify its customers positively.

I'm fairly confident that we will see more IT services being brought into the airline industry, not only on the ground, but also in the sky. Today, of course, you can make telephone calls and send emails from your airline seat, if you're willing to pay the price the airlines are charging. However, you can expect technology to drive these costs down, and, as a result, to see usage figures (and thus profitability figures) rise.

Boeing has had a long-term interest in equipping its aircraft with an "always-connected" sort of paradigm. In fact, a lot of research and development (R&D) is being done at Boeing, and a number of the airlines, too. This work includes putting high-speed fiber optic networks within planes and having those planes continuously connected through a satellite system that Boeing and others will launch. These efforts have been on hold, temporarily, for financial reasons, but, over time, expect to see continued work in this direction, particularly on long-haul flights.

It's also becoming clear that a lot of airlines' core transactional systems are getting a little bit long in the tooth. For example, if you look at the core of the SABRE airline system, it was all written in a very ancient IBM language. Of course, the difficulty here is that it would be very expensive to rewrite the code. Some rewrites were done in anticipation of Year 2000 (Y2K), but much work still needs to be done. SABRE, for example, checked more than 200 million lines of code to prepare for the Y2K transition. When these core transactional systems are finally redesigned, however, there will be a fantastic opportunity to consolidate the gains and the shifts in the way things have been done in the new frontend systems.

Over time, expect to see more and more functionality shift into these frontend systems while core backend transactional engines are redone as part of that core effort. This will allow folks in the airline industry to achieve greater operating efficiency and more flexibility going forward.

On another front, one of the things I learned by being involved in network design is that our U.S. hub-and-spoke system is not necessarily the most efficient routing protocol. I think the airlines have developed this heavy spoke system primarily for their own operational convenience and to "lock in" their customers. As a result, I think a whole wave of industry-wide redesign of the route structure is just waiting to be done.

It's going to take some solid scientific computing to reengineer the current route structures and to determine how to achieve better yields and efficiencies out of the system.

I hope that, over time, the FAA and other parts of the transportation industry will be examining these opportunities quite closely. Among the aforementioned suggestions are enormous opportunities for increasing profitability. Finally, I would like to mention that scientific work throughout the travel industry is likely to yield remarkable results in a number of additional areas that I didn't touch on in this chapter. For example, behold the words of noted political satirist, Mark Russell, who once said, "The scientific theory I like best is that the rings of Saturn are composed entirely of lost airline luggage."

So that's where my light blue polyester leisure suit and platform shoes have been hiding for all these decades!

Reengineering the Telecommunications Industry

Some folks think that *Citizen Kane* was the greatest movie ever made, but did you know that, in the race for the Academy Award for Best Picture in 1941, *Citizen Kane* "lost" to *How Green Was My Valley*?

Therefore, what's the difference between a winner and a loser? Well, the next time you run into famed director Steven Spielberg, you might want to ask him if he considers *Citizen Kane* to be a "winner" or a "loser." While you're at it, also don't forget to ask him if you can see Rosebud, the child's sled that played such a pivotal role in this Orson Welles film. Mr. Spielberg, you may remember, purchased the sled at auction recently with a "winning" bid of $55,000.

Speaking of winning bids, years ago, the governments of Europe and the United States decided to go into the wireless auction business to see if they could win themselves a pretty pocketful of change. Together, these governments generated almost $300 billion by selling wireless licenses for *four to five times* what they thought they were worth. Kind of makes your skin crawl, doesn't it? It was a time when everyone was caught up in the Internet frenzy, and cool, calm heads were definitely not prevailing.

The companies placing the "winning" bids thought that they were headed for the fast track to profit. Unfortunately, they paid outrageous sums for these rights, leaving these "winners" without any money to deploy their new wireless services. Many of these companies are now going bankrupt. What about the companies that "lost" the government auctions for wireless rights? They're now hoping to buy these licenses at reduced prices from our government's fire sale.

The moral of the story is that you can be the biggest "winner," even when you're the biggest "loser." So don't worry, Anna Kournikova. Although you've never "won" a major tennis tournament, being a "loser" is part of your lovely charm! Like some of the companies that lost the government auctions early on, I'm sure you're laughing all the way to the bank. (Those endorsement contracts sure are sweet.)

6.1 From Ostriches to Idiots

In the early days of the telecommunications industry, its leaders acted like ostriches. They just hid their heads in the sand, oblivious to the changing world around them. When they finally lifted their heads out of the sand, many of them began to act like idiots, taking themselves to the brink of extinction. Let this be a lesson to all of us.

If you look at the financial services industry or the travel industry, you'll see how they went through a widespread set of industry changes with sterling results. They even made their way through several rounds of deregulation without missing a beat. They did this by keeping their heads on straight, and, as a result, the financial services and travel industries have prospered.

The exact opposite can be said of the telecommunications industry. It had always been a stodgy industry. However, when a huge number of new entrants joined its ranks, all conventional wisdom was abandoned in favor of total insanity and idiocy. Herein lies a story from which we all can learn a great deal.

6.2 Monopoly Money

The telecommunications industry has always been utterly preoccupied with the physical laying of cable. Not only is this a very expensive endeavor, especially when it involves getting telecommunications lines out to individual subscribers, but it also has precluded the industry from paying attention to other, equally important, issues. For example, in the early days, there was drastic overcompetition in this industry. Private companies were springing up all over, and they all wanted to deliver telephone service to your home.

In urban areas, typically three or four providers were competing to wire the same house. Unhappy with their streets being torn apart to lay new cable, local government officials were in an uproar. They thought their neighborhoods could get by just fine with only one telephone line per house.

On the flip side, rural areas were being drastically underserved because it is very expensive to pull lines into these small communities.

Therefore, whereas competition was fierce in the cities, it was almost entirely nonexistent in outlying rural areas. This left the door wide open for the U.S. government to step in and establish some governing policies for the industry. The first thing our government did was to identify the telecommunications industry as a natural monopoly. This gave the government the power to regulate where various companies were allowed to deploy telephone service.

Next, our government came up with a set of very political cross-subsidy policies. The cross-subsidy policies were a reaction to the fact that telecommunications companies could pull a bundle of, say, 100 lines into a business a whole lot cheaper than they could string 100 separate lines into a residential area. However, due to government intervention, the cost *per line* of telephone service for businesses has been *double* the cost of residential service. This has resulted in an enormous cross-subsidy, wherein business users are subsidizing residential users. Similar logic was applied to having urban users subsidize rural users.

Next, in the 1990s, the U.S. government put into place a set of policies allowing for a cross-subsidy for schools and libraries. To pay for this subsidy, the government added an extra tax to all residential and business users' telephone bills. The tax was earmarked to connect schools and libraries to the Internet. Unfortunately, very little of that wiring has actually occurred, yet the taxes continue to be levied and collected.

All along, cities, states, and the U.S. government have had a huge amount of control over the telecommunication industry, and this regulatory infrastructure is probably the most Byzantine imaginable. Consider, for example, how many layers of regulatory intervention are involved in the telecommunications industry.

First of all, in the United States, cities regulate where telephone and cable lines can be pulled. They also regulate where fiber optics can be laid because these require easements to cross private property, and this requires use of the municipalities' rights of eminent domain. When lines cross public property, such as roads, companies are then required to pay franchise fees and to obtain permits.

On the next governmental level, phone rates have traditionally been regulated by the states. As you know, the states have authored a lot of regulatory policies that require business users' rates to subsidize residential users' rates. The residential users have simply had a lot more political clout on the state level than have business users, so the subsidies continue. These subsidies made sense in the early days of the industry, when governments were trying to promote the widespread deployment of telecommunications services and the cost of provisioning was high. In today's market, with drastically reduced costs of telecommunications services, they cause problems with deploying new technologies.

In addition, until recently, on the national level, the U.S. government proclaimed the telecommunications industry to be a natural monopoly, opening the door for sweeping regulatory restrictions and requirements. Businesses, in particular, were not enamored with all of the rules, regulations, and taxes that beset them, so they began to look for ways to ease the financial burden placed on them.

One of the steps businesses took to overcome their problems with the government's telecommunications policies was to adopt Private Branch Exchanges (PBXs). By modifying their existing telecommunications systems with PBXs, businesses could, in effect, buy their own telephone switches, which could be used for all calls made among their own employees within company walls. These PBXs allowed businesses to buy fewer outside telephone lines, which significantly reduced their overall phone expenditures. Instead of having to go back to a central switching center in an outside telephone company office, businesses could use PBX technologies to route internal calls themselves. This was supplemented with fiber optic technology, which has allowed businesses to buy phone lines in large, economic bundles.

These new bundles, or circuits, such as the T1 circuits, were originally designed to handle 24 telephone lines simultaneously. It didn't take long before businesses figured out that, if they were getting charged $30 a line by their local phone providers, they would be far better off operating a PBX, which would cost them only about $5 a line to operate.

Therefore, the race was on throughout the world to install PBX systems, and for very good reason. Rolm, in particular, was the company that pioneered the sale of PBX systems into enterprise accounts, and its business was on fire.

6.3 Bypass Surgery

Another way businesses started to save money on their phone bills was to buy T1 circuits directly from their long-distance providers, thereby bypassing their local exchanges altogether. HP, for example, still needed to have some lines into the local telecommunications environment, but it needed far more lines into a long-distance carrier. Performing bypass surgery on its telecommunications infrastructure was a masterstroke for HP. The company saved millions of dollars by making this change. No longer did it have to pay $30 or so a month for each of its telephone lines. By using bypass technology, HP bought only the number of local lines it needed for local traffic and then routed all of its other calls across a bypass line with its long-distance carrier. That's when MCI got into the game, which, by the way, proved to be very lucrative.

You may be wondering if the telecommunications industry tried to fight the attempt by businesses to bypass their oppressively expensive local exchanges. Did they ever! There were true knockdown, drag-out fights. The telecommunications industry claimed that, by allowing businesses to use PBXs, these businesses were using equipment that the industry had not certified to work on its network. They even claimed that uncertified, incompatible PBX equipment could shut down an entire telephone network.

Massive amounts of litigation followed, and we witnessed battle after battle, especially at the state level. There, the public utilities commissions were worried about the impact on large businesses if they weren't allowed to bypass their local exchanges for long-distance calls. These large businesses made a very persuasive argument that, if they weren't allowed to continue these practices in certain states, they would have to move to a more favorable environment somewhere else in the country. That, of course, would cause states to lose a lot of employees who were paying a lot in state taxes, which was something the public utilities commissions couldn't support.

As new technology allowed businesses to take control of their own communications destiny, the economic forces surrounding telephone fees got a little better balanced. This, in turn, helped the public utilities commissions, which before had been almost strictly consumer oriented, better understand the needs of business. State approval of bypass practices provided much relief to businesses that were already overburdened by the subsidies they were paying to lessen consumers' phone bills.

This is where you have to hand it to those clever folks at MCI. When all this turmoil was happening, they decided to build a parallel national network that allowed businesses to bypass their local carriers and to connect directly into them. MCI grew at a faster pace than anyone in the industry thought they would. However, businesses were fighting back from the mess of regulations they were under, and they were determined to win.

6.4 Now Entering the Ring: AT&T versus MCI

The telecommunications industry has typically used a 30-year depreciation cycle in its financial calculations: a cycle that was forced on them by the various public utilities commissions. In the past, when telephone companies have deployed capital equipment, they had to depreciate it across a 30-year period.

Meanwhile, in the late 1970s and early 1980s, digital equipment began replacing old analog equipment, and digital equipment has a lifecycle of about 5 years, not 30, like the old analog equipment. In addition, digital equipment has drastically lower maintenance and operation costs than the old copper switches that telephone companies used to install. Back in the 1960s and 1970s, a lot of telephone companies were still operating on mechanical switches with electromechanical relays. Unlike today's digital solutions, these mechanical devices were voracious consumers of power, hard to change, mechanically complex, and thus very expensive to operate.

When the very disruptive digital technologies arrived in the telecommunications industry in the late 1970s and early 1980s, MCI was ready to exploit this new technology in a big way, which scared AT&T to death.

Then, in the 1980s, in an effort to protect consumers and to foster more competition in the marketplace, the U.S. government stepped in and ordered the breakup of AT&T. It seemed as if the natural monopoly theory had just gone out of vogue with the U.S. government.

AT&T felt that MCI was cherry picking its biggest and most profitable customers. Because its local service lines were not particularly profitable, AT&T viewed the government breakup as a way to rid itself of its highly regulated local exchanges and focus instead on combating MCI for its most profitable, long-distance customers.

With the breakup of AT&T, a new breed of Regional Bell Operating Companies (RBOCs) was formed. These included, among others, PacBell, U.S. West, the NYNEX, Southwestern Bell, and Ameritech. These RBOCs basically took on the business of providing local phone service. In doing so, they also inherited all of the people who had expertise in dealing with state and local government regulation.

That left AT&T free to compete in a head-to-head battle with MCI. AT&T really had the scale and the resources to escalate this battle to a full-blown arms race. While AT&T and MCI were duking it out in the ring, along came another upstart called Sprint. Suddenly, what had been a pretty traditional fight became a real free-for-all.

Sprint, you see, came into the ring with the decided advantage of having access to about 30,000 miles of right-of-way along the old Southern Pacific Railroad tracks. What this meant was that the Sprint guys could lay a nationwide network of fiber optic lines because they already had access to the right of way.

It wasn't long before a number of companies were competing in the long-distance space. Notable entries included overlay carriers that were leasing lines in bulk from MCI, Sprint, and AT&T. These overlay carriers were then able to operate a virtual network on top of the physical network of the long lines providers. Their entry costs into the business were pretty low, making this quite the attractive opportunity for entrepreneurs.

What happened was that hundreds of long-distance overlay carriers sprang up. People were going through their switches, allowing the overlay carriers to bill for their services. Remember when every other commercial on television was for a 1-800-save-a-buck company? A lot of those companies haven't survived, but quite a few of them have prospered.

For businesses and consumers who made long-distance calls, this open competition has been fantastic. Rates for long-distance calls have plummeted to the point where you can call almost anywhere in the world for pennies a minute. Unfortunately, this has not held true for regional calls.

6.5 Meanwhile, Back at the Ranch...

Meanwhile, back at the ranch, the new RBOCs were working hard to achieve and maintain stability. Although saddled with a ton of old mechanical switches and other equipment, the RBOCs were also bringing in more electronic equipment. They weren't able to match the pace of the long-distance carriers in terms of deploying new technology, but the regional Bells were moving as quickly as they could, given the financial pressures they were experiencing. The 30-year depreciation cycles they inherited were an agonizing thorn in the sides of the baby Bells.

Seeking relief from the public utilities commissions, the RBOCs promoted something called incentive rate regulation, which they thought would improve their efficiency. They were hoping that the public utilities commissions would give them permission to invest in new equipment at a more rapid pace than they had traditionally done. In return, the RBOCs would enjoy huge operating cost savings that would ultimately benefit consumers. The baby Bells hoped to be able to pass along rate savings to their consumers, either by not raising rates or by actually reducing rates.

They were successful in their pleas for incentive rate regulation, and consumers really have benefited. If you look at the cost of acquiring local exchange service, it really hasn't gone up much over the years, and it certainly hasn't gone up at the rate of inflation. You can credit major new technology waves for these cost savings.

6.6 Wanting To Be in the Loop

In the 1970s and 1980s, we saw the wiring of the United States for cable TV. Phone companies were watching this with eager anticipation because they knew that it was possible to move telecommunications service across a cable TV infrastructure, particularly after that infrastructure moves to a digital framework. Although there are some problems with this approach, it has some promising features as well.

The phone companies also were looking for new sources of revenue, and delivering video services to homes looked particularly attractive. Some companies purchased cable TV properties, and others acquired direct broadcast wireless licenses and properties.

In the 1980s and 1990s, alternate ways of getting phone service all the way to consumers' homes became increasingly available. That last mile of service delivery had been quite the challenge before. The ability to reach that last mile happened, in part, due to the explosion in wireless technology. All of a sudden, you didn't need to lay cable or create a physical infrastructure to every home. That's the beauty of wireless technology.

With so many new ways to go that extra mile into the homes of consumers, the Federal Communications Commission (FCC) and various public utilities commissions have struggled with how they should regulate the local loop. Complicating this struggle was AT&T, which, in the 1990s, decided it wanted to get back into the local loop, which the company had exited when the government ordered the breakup of the telecommunications giant. However, AT&T was determined to get back in, especially as it started acquiring all of the cable TV properties that it could get its hands on. Then, AT&T started acquiring wireless properties.

It wasn't just AT&T that wanted back into the local loop. Powerful local companies across the nation were eyeing this opportunity and looking for ways to get their feet in the door as well. To the pleasure of many, a new round of government deregulation opened up the local loop to a host of new players. Urban areas were attractive targets for these companies, unlike rural areas that had all sorts of problems attracting service providers. However, today, thousands of independent telephone companies have stepped in to provide this service.

There is also another group of carriers known as Incumbent Local Exchange Carriers (ILECs). The primary driver behind these ILECs has been General Telephone & Electronics (GTE). GTE is the incumbent provider of service in parts of Texas, parts of the Northeast, and in many other parts of the nation. GTE is now part of Verizon, as you know. However, that's not all there is to this alphabet soup group of exchange carriers. Now, you have to add the new Competitive Local Exchange Carriers (CLECs) to the mix of RBOCs and ILECs. These are the folks who lease back circuits to another carrier to allow competitive service into local areas.

As you can see, the entire telecommunications landscape has turned into a crazy quilt of regulators and the regulated. To top off this incredible bowl of acronym soup, you have the Internet, which is going to dice the entire industry into little pieces.

6.7 The Internet Lures the Wild Guys

The core growth of the Internet happened because of MCI. This is because, at MCI, the Internet really became a reliable network for the very first time.

As you may recall, in the 1970s, a number of research networks were up and running. Typically, these networks ran on leased lines, such as 64-kilobit-per-second circuits. The major research universities in the country had leased a series of these circuits, which they used to build their networks, using protocols such as Transmission Control Protocol/Internet Protocol (TCP/IP). One of the largest networks (Bitnet) handled a huge, global email system for academic institutions.

Remember, T1 circuits had been built to bypass local exchanges and to resell unused telecommunications capacity in bulk. ATT developed the T1 to improve efficiency of the long haul network. Toward the mid-1980s, these T1 circuits enabled the construction of a permanent research network. The National Science Foundation (NSF), the Department of Energy (DOE), the Department of Defense (DOD), and DARPA collaborated to have this research network built.

The eventual winner was a company called Advanced Network and Services (ANS). There was a consortium of MERIT, IBM and MCI that bid and won the NSFNET backbone. Later the consortium was converted into a non-profit, Advanced Network and Services, the assets of which were later sold to AOL and WorldCom in a three-way swap. At this point, IBM owned part of MCI, and, because of that big investment, IBM was quite involved in the development of the world's first permanent Internet research network.

The initiative was lead by a former vice president in IBM's research organization, Al Weis. The plan was to have MCI provide the circuits for this initiative and Merit, Inc. to provide the operating hub. Al Weis and a core group of folks left IBM to work on this initiative. It was a gutsy move. Al and some key engineers left their good jobs at IBM to venture into the unknown. Along the way, coincidentally, IBM signed up to work on high-speed routing, which ultimately was going to be necessary to make the new Internet research network viable.

By the mid-1980s, the MERIT engineering team was able to put up a functioning, operational research network that succeeded far more than anyone ever dreamed it would. It was an amazing sight to behold. Within approximately 18 months, they migrated the T1 circuits to T3s, which increased the capacity of the network by 30 times practically overnight.

It was one heck of a race during that time just to keep up with the growing networking demand in the research community. Keep in mind that Al and his buddies were wild guys. They were certainly not part of the core network engineering team at MCI, although MCI did lend some very strong networking engineers to work on this initiative. However, Al and his team were willing to stick their necks out and to take on a whole lot of personal, professional, and technology risks. They were willing to push themselves and Internet technology to be the state of the art.

Eventually, the ANS network was sold to AOL, which used ANS's network capacity to help it scale up. The ANS network made $35 million from this sale ($10 million in cash and $25 million in stock). The network has continued to invest in other technology ventures to advance Internet technology and use and remains an influential not-for-profit venture. WorldCom did a deal involving AOL, Compuserve and ANS, wherein WorldCom got the core networks and AOL got the customer base.

People inside IBM hated Al. People inside MCI hated Al. However, at the end of the day, Al has proven again and again that he has very pure motives and one heck of a knack for taking his visions all the way through to fruition. A lot of people thought that he got an undeserved windfall when the ANS network was sold to AOL. I'm not among these naysayers. The fact of the matter is that he has done an incredible job behind the scenes moving Internet technology forward.

By the way, I know Al very well. He's a hard-driving character. However, for as long as I've known him, he's had the right vision, and he's had the drive to make things actually happen. Along the way, he's collected some incredible people to help him with his mission. These talented folks have provided incredible technical savvy, the purest of motives, and the long-term commitment necessary to succeed.

The telecommunications industry was downright stodgy until the mid-1980s. Then, when these wild guys and others came in from the outside, the industry was turned on its ear. There were some MCI and Sprint guys who were as wild as March hares. However, they really built these networks from the ground up and were exploiting Internet technologies far faster than AT&T was able to do during that era.

When IBM bought Rolm, a lot of the Rolm talent left because these guys were fast-paced entrepreneurs and were used to growing business opportunities rapidly and the associated thrill of swinging big deals. IBM was pretty stodgy at this stage, too, and there was a huge culture shock when Rolm came into the fold.

In fact, some of those Rolm guys formed the basis for the entrepreneurial talent behind Silicon Valley. They helped fuel the generation that enabled us to move from copper switching to electronic switching. They also helped prove that the stodgy, heavily regulated telecommunications industry could be operated in a more hands-off, entrepreneurial way.

6.8 Madness and Mayhem

By 1996, people were saying that they were seeing huge growth rates on the data side of their businesses. They didn't fully understand at this point how much of this growth was being driven by the Internet and how much was just being driven by data needs in general.

At the time, there were lots of IBM's Systems Network Architecture (SNA) protocol networks out there. With this protocol, you could build very powerful private networks. Banks, in particular, were having SNA networks built for them in large numbers. These networks had much higher security than did the Internet, and they also were much more efficient for moving data.

Lots of private SNA networks were out there. IBM started two of these as joint ventures with Sears. One was Prodigy, and the other was Advantis, a data network business. From its early days, Advantis was doing about $2 to $3 billion a year. The data business was growing by leaps and bounds, and the Advantis gang really knew how to exploit this opportunity.

Remember back to 1995 and 1996, when the automotive industry jumped on the Internet bandwagon? The industry did this instead of extending its SNA networks. The auto industry was much more interested in linking its supply and distribution chains than it was in linking heavy transaction systems.

Meanwhile, the airline industry had moved to X.25 (a standard protocol suite developed to describe how data passes into and out of public data communications networks), which it soon found didn't scale up very well; beyond that, multiple applications didn't support X.25 in any sophisticated way.

Therefore, a massive race by corporations started in 1995 and 1996 to shift their networks to the Internet Protocol (IP). It was at this time that telecommunications providers were seeing their leased-line business doubling every three to four months. At the same time, we saw early experiments with transmitting voice across the TCP/IP network, so it was clear that the digital revolution was sweeping through the telecommunications industry.

When you make a telephone call from your home, your conversation is typically digitized at the switch. From there, digital packets are sent out across the voice network. By the time your voice arrives at the other end of the phone call, it returns to an analog format.

Today, companies like Rolm and Nortel provide end-to-end digital service, and many PBX systems have been converted to an all-digital format. The telephone itself was actually used to do the digitization. Voice, as it's transmitted today, is digitized in some fashion after it enters the network.

For many years, there has been the dream of convergence among those working in the telecommunications industry. This convergence lovefest really hit its stride in the telecommunications industry during 1996 and 1997. The idea was that the industry was going to build unified networks that would handle voice, video, and data. That dream was the driving force behind all of the acquisitions that AT&T was doing at that time.

At the industry meeting I attended in 1996, however, the executives generally agreed that it would still be another five to seven years before they needed to worry seriously about convergence. For the most part, they agreed with each other that data didn't account for much in terms of their revenues, so the urgency to pay attention to it just wasn't there.

Big mistake. Monumental mistake.

The crossover point came between 1998 and 1999, when the raw traffic for the Internet exceeded the raw traffic for voice. By 2001, the revenues from data traffic exceeded the revenues from voice traffic. Complicating this formula is the fact that the profit per packet is dramatically less for data than it is for voice.

Then, in the late 1990s, Dense Wave Division Multiplexing (DWDM) came along. This technology allowed the actual splitting of light beams that travel down fiber optic cables. Each of the new multiple frequencies can carry as much data as the entire frequency spectrum carried before. In effect, a single fiber optic cable could end up with 32 times the capacity it previously had. With this new generation of fiber optic cable, we've been able to put up to 1,000 channels on a single fiber. That has been a major breakthrough in carrying capacity for long-haul fibers.

Therefore, companies like MCI and Sprint that had earlier deployed nationwide fiber network, were all of a sudden enjoying capacity they never dreamed possible before, all at an incredibly low cost, due to DWDM. In addition, companies like Qwest and Level3, as well as other companies like Williams Communications and International X.25 Interconnect (IXI), exploited existing rights of way to deploy all-new fiber optic networks. With all this newly found capacity, what were these telecommunications companies going to do with it? Well, for one thing, it sure was going to come in handy as they needed extra bandwidth for the Internet.

At this same time, there were some major breakthroughs in the routing industry. One of the key breakthroughs was what we call wire speed routing. Wire speed routing allows us to move TCP/IP packets effectively across the network, essentially at the speed of the underlying network. Today, wire speed routing can move bits at the speed of the underlying Synchronous Optical Network (SONET), or 768 times as fast as the second generation DS3 (digital signal with a transmission rate of 44.736 megabits per second) Internet. Keep in mind that this capacity is available for each of the new channels provided by DWDM.

Because of these disruptive technologies on the data side of the equation, we're now able to move massive amounts of data across long-haul networks at a much lower cost per packet than the cost of moving voice.

The sticky wicket of this situation occurs in the last mile loop. That's where the telecommunications industry has had some major problems both in its convergence vision and in the economics of the industry. The muddled mess has been complicated by the entry into this industry by yet a new generation of companies, among which was Enron. Yes, Enron was part of this growing fiasco.

Global Crossing, which has now filed for bankruptcy, hired the chief networking engineer for undersea cables from AT&T. This fellow went to a Wall Street banker and told him that he believed that there was a huge under-served market for transoceanic cables, particularly to Europe, and he was right. When he was still at AT&T, this chief networking engineer couldn't get the attention of AT&T because it was preoccupied with buying wireless and cable properties while neglecting the wholesale market for traffic across the ocean. However, unlike AT&T, Global Crossing was paying attention. Global Crossing bought MCI's undersea cable maintenance fleet. Then, it pulled a ton of brand new fiber optic cables from the U.S. to Europe.

The reason this is important is that the previous generation of trans-oceanic cables was so old that their repeaters were not capable of carrying DWDM traffic. Therefore, suddenly, the new Global Crossing fiber pro-vided dramatically improved capacity that had simply not been there before, and the cost of delivering it was incredible. Global Crossing was able to pay back its total investment in its undersea cable in a period of under a year.

The European crossing was a brilliant success. Because of that, and the fact that capital was so easy to obtain, Global Crossing decided to get into the business of laying fiber optic cable on a massive scale. In fact, its vision was to wrap the globe in about 100,000 miles of fiber optic cable. The prob-lem was that Global Crossing was counting its subsidiaries before they hatched, which was a key factor in the company's financial troubles.

Meanwhile, on terra firma, Qwest was launching a plan of its own. Remember that the Qwest guys got access to the Southern Pacific right of way? Well, they also hired a stable of former Sprint engineers who had pre-viously deployed the Sprint network. These brainy, newly hired engineers deployed a new, patented trenching machine for Qwest. This trenching machine featured a sled that straddled the Southern Pacific tracks and dropped a bundle of 96 pairs of fiber optic cables as it whizzed down the tracks at 35 miles an hour. Within a period of just 18 months, Qwest was able to build the best nationwide fiber optic network in the country. In fact, it was so successful in the United States that Qwest then went to Europe and built the same kind of network there with its Dutch partner, KPN.

Enter Level3 into this mix. It was Level3's idea to deploy big, high-capacity conduits and to blow fiber through the conduits just when it was needed. This would allow Level3 to use the latest generation fiber technology. Level3's strategy was to have a continuously upgradeable capacity for its conduits.

At this stage, Qwest, Level3, and Global Crossing were all survivors, but, by January 2002, Global Crossing filed for bankruptcy. My feeling is that Global Crossing will be able to survive because it has some great assets, but it will have to do some serious reorganizing.

Part of the problem that Global Crossing had was that it set up global hosting centers close to the hubs of their major networks. Global Crossing would then go to big corporations and suggest that these companies host right on the network to take advantage of the new bandwidth capabilities. That is what started to sink Global Crossing. The folks at the hosting operations have not been able to get the labor breakthroughs that they need. IBM has done a good job of this, but everyone else has struggled. Exodus is bankrupt. Global Crossing sold its property to Exodus at a huge loss, and Qwest has been losing its shirt on its hosting centers.

Compounding the problem was the fact that these companies were trying to get into the business of becoming broader carriers. Qwest acquired U.S. West, and this hasn't turned out to be the profitable acquisition that Qwest had hoped it would be. Global Crossing acquired Frontier Telecommunications, an ILEC company. Interestingly, Frontier leased one-fourth of the Qwest Network. An incestuous, and particularly profitable, crazy quilt had been formed.

Now, the wireless folks stepped in, thinking that they would be the answer to the local loop problem. However, the challenge here is that wireless technologies don't handle data very well, and their links operate at very low speeds. Compounding the problem is that wireless voice quality is not particularly good because wireless connections operate at less than 20 kilobits per second. You couldn't even find a modem that operates that slowly today.

Yet hope springs eternal. In future 3G environments, we'll be able to live in an always-connected, wireless world, or so they say. The data capacity for this new network could go up to 3 megabits per second, which is far faster than the average consumer accesses the Internet today. At this speed, wireless networks will be able to carry near-broadcast quality video.

However, wouldn't you know it? The government has decided to jump in and auction off wireless licenses. As I mentioned at the beginning of this chapter, our government anticipated that these auctions would yield only $60 to $75 billion. However, a bidding frenzy occurred, and companies eager to own these new wireless licenses jacked up the price to almost $300 billion.

Of course, after these companies spent all of their assets on acquiring these licenses, they had nothing left to deploy the wireless services on which they banked their futures. Unfortunately, that's a story we've seen before with other "winning" companies. Today, many of these overpriced licenses are now in the hands of the government again because the first set of bidders were unable to pay for what they won in the auctions.

Sooner or later, though, this is all going to sort itself out. The license problem will get solved. Hopefully, we'll still have a few companies left that are solvent and still have an appetite to make some capital investments so that we can actually get these new wireless services deployed.

Ironically, the original losers of the wireless auction bidding war are going to survive, but many of the strongest companies have been taken out of the competition. For example, KPN, the Dutch telephone company, is probably the most technologically savvy telephone company in Europe, yet it has been effectively removed from the wireless race because it won too many wireless auctions. This kind of thing scares me because I just don't think we can afford to lose the talent we have in this industry.

6.9 Unraveling the Tangled Web

Looking forward, I see massive consolidation ahead for the telecommunications industry. Right now, Europe and the United States have very fragmented markets, and we're already seeing consolidation, as in the recent Bell Atlantic and NYNEX merger. The same thing applies to Qwest because it has acquired U.S. West. My guess is that we've only seen the tip of this merger iceberg.

Somebody, sooner or later, is going to have to take a look at this industry from a regulatory point of view and unravel the tangled mess we've gotten ourselves into with all the cross-subsidies and multiple tiers of regulation. All of that needs to be harmonized so that we can deliver predictable results in the telecommunications industry.

Beyond that, the industry has been disrupted by major waves of new technology, yet there has not been a clean way of bringing new technologies into the industry. Too many regulatory roadblocks are going to have to be removed before this industry can wire itself for the future.

Unlike the automotive and airline industries that brought the assimilation of new technology to a science, the telecommunications industry has tried to assimilate technology with a level of idiocy not seen before in this new world.

There are a few bright spots out there. The RBOCs, for example, have had a pretty steady drumbeat of profitability because of the rate regulations they've been under. RBOCs haven't been given the government incentives to deploy the most advanced technology on a systematic basis. This is eventually going to catch up with them because the RBOCs have a long, long way to go, technologically speaking. A few RBOCs have been reasonably good because they've had extraordinary leadership teams, but others have been just terrible about deploying new technology.

There are some very important lessons we can learn from the telecommunications industry and apply to our business situations. Among them are the following:

- You must thoroughly understand the available technology.
- You must have a skilled team of people who know how to best deploy the technology.
- You must have a solid vision of the results you want to deliver, both from a technological and business point of view.
- You must have a relentless operating discipline.

The global telecommunications industry generates revenues of almost $1 trillion a year. This makes it the world's single largest industry. In fact, if this industry were a country, it probably would be 14th or 15th in the world in terms of Gross Domestic Product (GDP).

And yet it struggles.

Because the entry barriers are so high and due to the capital costs needed to participate in this industry, many have hesitated to join its ranks. However, many major technology breakthroughs are ahead, and these will entice a wealth of new and capable players in the future.

This has been an industry that has been more disrupted by technology than almost any other. In addition, it has been burdened by a regulatory structure that dates back a full century.

Compounding the challenges faced by the telecommunications industry is that fact that it now has to deal with fundamental shifts in its revenue base. The less-regulated wireless business is likely to pick up even more market share as time progresses. Also, as I mentioned earlier, the revenue from data is now larger than it is from voice.

In addition, the unnatural dance between the regulators and the regulated is causing major problems for the telecommunications industry. Among them is the inability of the industry to establish a rational, long-term, and focused way to absorb technology at a reasonable pace, in a way it can afford, and in a manner that benefits its customers.

One can only hope that the oppressive grip of government regulation is loosened so this industry can once again thrive. A positive step in that direction will occur if more reasonable heads prevail during the second round of bidding for wireless auctions.

Finally, speaking of auctions, have you ever wondered what the largest winning bid was at a Sotheby's auction? Well, it occurred on May 10, 1999, when Sotheby's conducted the bidding process for Paul Cezanne's work, *Rideau, Cruchon Et Compotier*. It was estimated that the final selling price going into the auction would be between $25 and $35 million, but the final hammer price, with the buyer's premium, was $60,502,500.

Impressive, yes, but Christie's can top even that astonishing figure. In 1990, a Japanese businessman paid $82.5 million at a Christie's auction for Vincent van Gogh's painting, *Portrait of Dr. Gachet*.

I wonder how many wireless licenses (or shares of a single license) that sum could yield in the years ahead....

CHAPTER 7

The Great Eyeball Race

When Alexander Graham Bell invented the telephone in 1875, he actually was trying to invent a talking telegraph. His associate, Thomas Watson, fashioned the device we now know as the telephone, by assembling a wooden stand, a funnel, a cup of acid, and some copper wire into a contraption that would carry sound over a long distance.

And before you could say, "Mr. Watson, come here. I want to see you," the Great Eardrum Race was on.

On March 7, 1876, Bell received his first telephone patent, and that was the beginning of the Bell Telephone Company. By 1881, every major city and town in the United States had its own telephone exchange. Everybody who was *anybody* had a phone.

However, the real floodgates for this new technology didn't open until Bell's second telephone patent expired in 1894. From that moment forward, and for the next 10 years, more than six thousand telephone companies sprang up in this country, and the number of working telephones skyrocketed from 285,000 to 3,317,000.

Does this ring a familiar bell with any of you? If not, allow me, please, to dial you in....

Just about one hundred years later, when the Internet went public in 1995, our own generation's technology floodgates were opened, and the Great Eyeball Race was on. Fasten your seatbelts ladies and gentlemen. This is going to be a bumpy ride.

7.1 Reach Out and Touch Someone

When the Internet went public in 1995, tens of thousands of enterprising folks rushed down this new primrose path to profitability. The theory was that, if you could get enough eyeballs looking at your new Web site, somehow serious revenues and profits magically would appear at your doorstep.

The first successful forays into delivering content on networks were adjuncts to traditional publishing in professional fields. For example, Lexis-Nexis delivered a variety of services to lawyers, accountants, and doctors, and Westlaw offered a competitive service. Early versions of these services bundled in network access, a workstation, and a monthly subscription.

These businesses made a go of it because they had high value content and lots of it. Professionals were now able save countless hours of tedious effort, thanks to their newfound ability to do textual searches of this content. Even though lower-cost clerks and paraprofessionals performed much of the research, it was still costly, highly skilled work.

Before 1995, three very popular online services were available: CompuServe (a subsidiary of H&R Block), AOL (which was in its infancy at that point and not Internet based), and Prodigy (which was an IBM-Sears joint venture). In the mid-1990s, Prodigy was the largest of the three online services.

The folks at H&R Block had powerful centralized computers that they used during tax season, but, during the off-season, which made up most of their year, these computers sat idle. Such a waste. That's when some of the brightest H&R Block folks came up with an ingenious idea for putting these computers to good use. They started a subsidiary called CompuServe, a company focusing on providing content to professionals.

CompuServe, AOL, and Prodigy were what we call today "walled gardens," environments in which people work in communities and access online services in a prepackaged way. People were signing up for these services in droves. Within a couple of years, millions of subscribers were using CompuServe, AOL, and Prodigy and forming reasonably large communities in those environments.

CompuServe tended to be more business oriented than the other services. Interestingly, Prodigy became a consumer-oriented company, and it was among the first of the companies to adopt Web-based family fare and services.

When Steve Case joined AOL, he brought with him a very strong consumer focus that he acquired when he was a top executive at Proctor & Gamble. One of the first things he did as Chief Operating Officer (CEO) of AOL was to hire a seasoned executive team with a fair amount of media and entertainment experience. The vision and flair of these executives can be seen in the user-friendly interfaces and the myriad family services that AOL offers.

Prodigy quickly discovered that one of its most promising sources of profitability could be found among its online communities, so Prodigy threw a great deal of resources into developing its user communities. CompuServe, on the other hand, focused its attention on developing content. It had lots of databases containing professional content, and millions of users were accessing this information. CompuServe was making a pretty penny by charging its users a premium for accessing various services. AOL also was charging for its premium services, but it quickly discovered that additional revenue streams could be gleaned from its user communities.

As the Internet caught fire, Microsoft also joined the gravy train by introducing its own online service, MSN. Microsoft's entry into this arena was seen as a huge threat to the entire industry. Many thought Microsoft's pre-existing grip on the eyeballs of so many millions of people on their desktops would threaten the very openness of the Internet. MSN was viewed as such a powerful player in this arena because many thought that Microsoft could leverage its desktop monopoly to connect people, more or less automatically, to its online property. There, the second round of significant antitrust activity lodged against Microsoft began.

Remember, too, that computer manufacturers were earning revenues from the online service companies. By including the icons of AOL or CompuServe or Prodigy on their desktops, computer manufacturers were making it easy for people to sign up for these services, and the online services were paying the manufacturers "bounties" for including their icons and software on their systems.

As I mentioned in Chapter 5, all sorts of folks in this industry were up in arms about the early and unfair advantages American Airlines had created for itself by programming its SABRE system to favor American Airlines routes over competitor routes. American Airlines was quick to remedy this situation gracefully, to the utter delight and relief of the rest of the airline industry.

The same cannot be said about Microsoft's approach to its MSN network. Microsoft continued to push computer manufacturers to have its icon first, foremost, and forever on as many computer monitors as possible, while insisting on having all other logos hidden from view.

There was a fair amount of litigation and threatened litigation, and some fascinating jockeying for position at this time. Nevertheless, because AOL, CompuServe, and Prodigy were already online, they were well positioned to give Microsoft a run for its money. Although these three companies changed their business models to one of providing Internet services, the great eyeball race with MSN was underway, and this was a race that was going to be undertaken with a vengeance, I might add.

I should point out that the business models being pursued looked a lot like traditional publishing models, only with a different distribution mechanism and faster ramp times. These models are basically subscriptions subsidized with advertising. On the Internet, the process of getting subscriptions happens at a much faster pace, the market is more global, and the physical delivery problems are reduced. On the other hand, the revenue sources are the same as for conventional publishing. This has been an extremely stable business model for more than one hundred years. The model is basically a steady, recurring revenue base (subscriptions) with a more opportunistic upside (advertising).

7.2 Fishing for Eyeballs

When the Internet took off, I used to joke with my fellow IBM executives about how this new phenomenon reminded me of the story about the blind man and the elephant. In those early days, wherever consumers first touched the Internet, like wherever the blind man first touched the elephant, that initial point of contact formed the basis for how they thought the entire Internet looked and operated. There was virtually no understanding on the part of consumers regarding how enormous and powerful the Internet actually was or would become. More important, it seemed that most executives, from whatever industry, now viewed the Internet through the eyes of their recent consumer experience. They also blindly adopted portions of the business models pioneered by online service providers.

When I joined HP, I noticed that my new colleagues also suffered from the blind man and the elephant syndrome. Most HP executives had lots of impressive experience, but just not with the full scope and potential of the Internet. Therefore, their understanding of the Internet was often based on their experiences with the Internet as consumers only. Therefore, to a whole lot of IBM and HP executives, the whole Internet spelled out "e-y-e-b-a-l-l r-a-c-e."

According to the eyeball-race theory, the new dot.coms could grow their businesses in ways that paralleled the adoption curves of the telephone, broadcast TV, and cable TV. Advertisers considered that 30 to 35 million subscribers would represent critical mass, and, after the Internet reached this level, it would automatically become a viable advertising media.

The Internet hit that milestone around 1996. This achievement then fueled the hope that, all of a sudden, advertisers would start dumping massive advertising dollars into various Web sites. Online service providers, on the other hand, continued to build their businesses with the proven newspaper model: subscriptions subsidized by advertising.

Then Yahoo came along with a very interesting value proposition. Even at this early stage of the public Internet, there was an enormous amount of content out on the Internet. Yahoo theorized that it could build a very successful business by hosting a site on which all of these millions of pages of Web content could be accessed in a clear, simple, and rapid fashion. Revenue was generated primarily through advertising without recurring subscription revenue. This added further fuel to the great eyeball race, and the race for content. Dreams of dollar signs were consuming everyone, everywhere.

A whole new generation of businesses centered on content packaging, and search engines sprang up, mostly fueled by advertising revenue. Because start-up costs and times for online businesses are dramatically less than for physical businesses, in no time at all, this segment of the market became overserved. All you ever heard about during this period was "dot.com this and dot.com that," and, before you knew it, the Internet was besieged by unorganized content that was increasing exponentially.

That's when Yahoo! came to the rescue with a tremendous new business model designed to unscramble the tangled Web we had woven. Yahoo! didn't own its connectivity function, nor was it getting subscriptions, but it did get lots of "hits." However, Yahoo! was racking up very impressive advertising revenues, and, all of a sudden, it was one of the darlings of the dot.com era.

The technology behind Yahoo! was pretty simple. The underlying genius behind its business strategy was to make the Internet usable for the average person. At one stage, Yahoo! had hundreds of librarians cataloging the Internet. Their work formed the basis for the search engine that Yahoo! was building, an engine that would tame the Internet and make it useable for average human beings.

For early users, particularly in 1995 through 1997, their first pit stop on the Internet would likely be the Yahoo! site. A whole lot of eyeballs were falling into the lap of Yahoo!, and Microsoft watched, studied, and salivated.

Not to be outdone by Yahoo!, the Microsoft team had a plan up its sleeve. Its vision was that every time anyone in the world would turn on a computer, the first thing that would appear on the screen would be the Microsoft logo or the MSN logo. In either case, consumers would come face to face with Microsoft each time they tapped the ON button on their computers.

Netscape also wanted to be part of this eyeball race, so it began shipping its browser with a very handy entry button into the Web. All of a sudden, Netscape had a truckload of eyeballs, too.

However, for a long time, Netscape couldn't quite figure out how to leverage those eyeballs. This made Netscape a prime takeover target for AOL, whose traditional walled-garden strategy could be greatly enhanced by the acquisition of Netscape's millions of pure Internet users. Again, the prospect of dollar signs enticingly flashed before the eyes of AOL's executives.

Therefore, here we had AOL, Netscape, MSN, Yahoo!, and CompuServe, and the gold rush for advertising dollars was on. Yahoo! became profitable very quickly. With only a modest investment up front, Yahoo! was able turn a profit without having to do all of the value-added packaging that AOL had to do.

There was a perception in the marketplace that the entry barriers for doing business on the Internet were much lower than those in traditional business environments. However, Microsoft spent billions of dollars building MSN, and AOL spent billions building its business. Conversely, with very little upfront investment, Yahoo! came on the scene, and, right out of the chute, it was making money hand over fist.

During this time, there was also a great Internet real estate land rush. The theory of this model was that the opening of the Internet frontier was like the opening of the American West, where people rushed to file homestead claims. In the case of the Internet, the homestead claims were "captured retail mindshare" in particular product categories. There was a rush to file for Internet addresses like "toys.com," "furniture.com," "groceries.com," and so on. The logic went that, because Amazon.com had captured so much mindshare so quickly, that there would only be room in the market for one or two big companies and that the early movers would dominate their respective marketspaces. Of course, now we have Borders.com, Dalton.com, and so forth.

The problem on the Internet is that the communications channel is open to all comers for very modest investments. If the business has a good basic operations model, taking it to the Internet is a relatively fast and uncomplicated effort, as evidenced by the new "click and mortar" sites. If the only thing a company has is a dot.com address, building a real business behind it can be quite a challenge.

For companies fortunate enough to have their value propositions perpetuated in the industry, continuously enhancing those value propositions has been an ongoing challenge. Yahoo! has skillfully met this challenge with such moves as acquiring hotjobs.com. The more narrowly based providers have had a hard time holding onto their subscribers, and thus their advertising revenue.

As investors continued to fish for eyeballs, several entrepreneurs ventured into the niche categories of bidding wars and spot markets. Priceline.com, eBay, and other similar sites appeared with such voracity that the whole wired world began looking like an auction. The problems many of these sites encountered were that "no-bargain" bargains are easier to sniff out, and unreliable delivery or deliverers undermine the value of the exchanges.

7.3 The Slippery Slope from Dot.Com to Dot.Bomb

In January 2002, Amazon.com announced its first quarterly profit. This was huge news despite the fact that Amazon only made a penny a share. At last, Amazon, a dot.com company, had found a way to get its operations under control, and its huge investments were starting to pay off. Interestingly, one of the fastest growing and most profitable areas of Amazon's business is in helping other companies get online. As a result, its professional services organization has turned itself into a huge moneymaker for Amazon.

Well, before Amazon turned a profit, however, thousands of hungry entrepreneurs were watching its every move, and trying to figure out how they could sell everything from soup to nuts over the Internet. They were especially drooling over the prospect of not having to build a big and costly retail network in order to do retail sales over the Internet.

However, traditional retailers also were eyeing the Internet with eager anticipation. Many of these retailers had been experiencing moderate success in their efforts to sell their products, not only in their stores, but also by means of 1-800 numbers. Much to their delight, many of these traditional retailers were able to move fairly quickly into the realm of online Internet sales. Coincidentally, in 1996 and 1997, there were a number of relatively decent Internet products coming on the market, which made it easier for retailers to put up their electronic storefronts.

IBM was doing a lot of work in this space by offering its Open Market product, which represented the beginning of its very successful e-business initiative. IBM was helping to establish the interfaces that allowed companies to actually sell things over the Internet and to accept payment for these products.

At the same time, a new SSL protocol was introduced and accepted by credit card companies, retailers, and consumers, and, all of a sudden, this new avenue of commerce received a significant boost. The SSL is what ensures secure Internet sites and the ability to transmit information safely. Now, companies could actually sell items reasonably well over the Internet.

Amazon got a toehold in the door quickly because it already had a book distribution warehouse. As you may know, the book business is a tough business because retailers expect to return a fair amount of unsold books to the warehouses. (I humbly hope that such will not be the case for this, my first book!)

At any rate, the Amazon folks were lucky enough to come across a warehousing operation, which they purchased and leveraged to their great advantage from a retailing point of view. Amazon was also technologically skilled and able to apply this talent by creating a very inviting, broad catalogue of online books, accompanied by a fantastic search engine that could deliver customers to their favorite book choices in the blink of an eye. Next, Amazon focused on the rapid delivery of its products, each of which was offered at a fairly good price. Customers loved this experience, and they were buying books from Amazon at an incredible rate.

I remember visiting one venture capital company in 1997, and I literally discovered that every venture-funded activity it was launching was for an online retailer. I remember scratching my head and thinking, "Hasn't this venture capital firm realized that it is going to have huge transportation problems with some of the online retail operations it is starting?"

For example, the firm was funding online furniture companies. Imagine the logistics problems involved when customers would order a couch online, have it shipped to their homes, and then decide they didn't like what was sent because it was damaged in transit, or the fabric wasn't as expected or the color looked awful. How on earth would a customer prepare a couch for return shipment? The business model for customer returns would be a nightmare, which was one of the reasons why Furniture.com tanked.

Obviously, other products and services were better suited for an online environment. Consider online matchmaking, which has become a very big business. It's surprising how many true romances have blossomed over the Internet. There is no shortage of remarkable stories about people meeting each other that way and then falling in love and marrying.

On the steamy side of the Internet, I recall from my days at IBM that we made a Top 10 List which we were not particularly proud of. This was back in 1996, and *Penthouse* magazine had just published a list of the top corporations in America whose employees were accessing its Web site by using their corporate accounts. Imagine our shock and embarrassment when IBM showed up on that list.

What resulted was a very rapid education effort across IBM about the appropriate use of company resources. It reminded me of my earlier days at Indiana University, when we had Internet usage problems of a similar nature.

Anyway, at IBM, we knew we had a challenge on our hands. If we put a filter on our computer systems at work, we'd undoubtedly end up in the newspapers the next day, with headlines like "IBM Filters *Penthouse*." Therefore, our objective was two-fold: first, to educate our employees, and, second, to stay out of the press.

As it turned out, IBM did a nice job of stressing to its employees the importance of getting their online activity under control. Hits to the *Penthouse* site by IBM employees tapered off, and IBM quietly clamped a smut filter on its internal systems. I suspect that more than one company has faced this challenge in the Internet age.

The wacky world of online enterprises also included the curious entry of groceries into the market. The delivery problems with perishable commodities, as you can imagine, were a nightmare. However, people somehow thought that, because their groceries were being sold on the Internet, all of the basic rules of economics (for example, you shouldn't mix a low-margin business with an additional high-cost delivery model) were suspended. These online grocery operations had such a preoccupation with the retail experience they were delivering to their customers on their Web sites that they failed to focus on the entire delivery chain necessary to get the products from their warehouses to their customers' front doors.

Then, sites like eBay sprang up, and online auctions began to capture the attention of consumers. The beauty of these sites was that they made it possible for individuals to put items up for bid without having to create an underlying commerce infrastructure. It was an ingenious entry into the online world.

By 1998, conventional retailers started coming into the Web in a more meaningful fashion. Amazon's professional services organization was right there to help these folks establish their online presence. The nice thing about having conventional retailers on the Web was that a lot of the logistical problems were solved right out of the gate. For example, if a customer ordered a blouse from Nordstrom.com and it didn't fit, the customer could easily return it to a nearby retail outlet, rather than having to mess with mailing it back. All of a sudden, traditional brick and mortar companies were finding success as click and mortar companies.

Success was achieved because these folks began to think through all of the aspects of delivery and the total customer experience, not just the purchasing experience, as so many dot.coms had done before.

All in all, we were seeing a lot of folks taking their business to the Internet, dreaming about their forthcoming riches, and, more often than not, discovering that, if they were going to be successful, they were going to have to *earn* their money. It wasn't going to fall into their laps.

It is interesting that *The Producers* should be the top Broadway show in 2001. This old film classic, written and produced by Mel Brooks, is the perfect model for much of the dot.com industry. The theory behind *The Producers* is that, if you produce a flop, the investors will just write off their monetary losses and you can simply oversubscribe the production. To a large extent, the "dot.bombs" were more focused on "going public" than they were on building businesses. Most of the dot.bombs were lavishly spending someone else's money, and this applied to companies large and small.

7.3.1 Bomb #1: A Lack of Conventional Promotional Activities

During the late 1990s, too many marketing folks were thinking that all they had to do was create a presence on the Internet and instantly they would be making barrels and barrels of money. People were thinking, "Build it, and they will come!" What went wrong? Why did so many dot.com companies slide down the slippery slope to the world of dot.bombs?

First of all, a lot of dot.coms discovered that getting customers was harder than they thought. They were under the mistaken impression that all they had to do was put up a site and customers would magically appear. The lesson to be learned here is that it still takes promotion through conventional means to attract customers.

Steve Case knew this lesson well from his days at Proctor & Gamble. He instinctively knew how to reach customers. In fact, there was a joke going around recently about Steve Case and AOL. It went something like this: "Why is Steve Case upset that they've discovered life on Mars? Because now he has to figure out how to get an AOL CD up there!"

You've got to hand it to Steve, though. He has blanketed this country with AOL CDs, offering free hours on AOL. The CDs come in newspapers. They're delivered with the mail. They pop up in magazines. Steve Case is a consumer guy, and he sure knows how to promote his product. Believe me, he uses every conceivable conventional means at his disposal to promote AOL to consumers.

The funny thing is that most folks would agree that Prodigy and CompuServe had better products than AOL; they just hadn't mastered the marketing formula the way Steve Case had, which is what really distanced AOL from the pack. Steve just knew how to promote to consumers, and, as his installed base at AOL increased, he made additional investments in improved programming.

If you are considering taking your business to the Internet, I urge you to avoid one of the prime pitfalls experienced by the dot.bombs. They dramatically underestimated their customer procurement costs.

7.3.2 Bomb #2: Too Narrow a Value Proposition

The second major problem that many of the dot.bombs had was that they had too narrow a value proposition. They figured that customers were going to come to their sites magically, and, because so many people were flocking to the Internet, they could offer a very narrow value proposition and still get to a critical mass. Big mistake.

It's true that today's sophisticated search engines can lead customers to precisely the kinds of things they want, no matter how specialized these things might be. However, what happened from a business model point of view is that a lot of these dot.bombs assumed that their niches were going to be a lot larger than they actually ended up being.

The most successful players in the niche markets understood how to promote themselves and how to make sure that the various search engines out there would pick up their sites and drive customers to their doors. That required spending promotional dollars, just like it did in the physical universe.

Take a look at AOL. One of the things it has done so well over time is to continue to enhance its offerings. For example, right now AOL is adding digital imaging services, photo services, and similar products to its customer portfolio.

As you know, through its entire history, AOL has continued to add value to its bundle of services. Their purpose in doing that has been to keep customers loyal and to keep them paying that monthly subscription fee. It generally has been more cost-effective for AOL to design and introduce new services than it has been for it to offer a price reduction in its subscription fees.

The challenge for online service providers has been to hold their prices steady while continuing to add more value. Luckily, as the cost of computing and storage continues to fall, online service providers have been able to reinvest those cost savings into enhancing their services.

If you look at Amazon's Web site, you'll notice that it continues to evolve and expand its customer experience. This strategy has allowed Amazon to grow its retail base without dramatically adding to the capital costs of running the business. Of course, as Amazon has expanded, the logistics of fulfillment have gotten to be a gigantic nightmare.

7.3.3 Bomb #3: An Inadequate Delivery Chain

The third problem for the dot.bombs involved the monumental task of product delivery. Whenever these companies touched the physical universe in any way, unique delivery challenges arose. Whereas AOL is largely a consumer "experience," many dot.com folks had to worry about transporting their physical products from one location to another. The logistics involved in this endeavor were enormous.

A lot of companies that attempted to sell groceries and other perishables, and larger items such as furniture over the Internet ended up bombing. Factors such as road conditions, weather conditions, product availability, and the nightmare of product returns were all wreaking havoc on the balance sheets of some of these early dot.bomb companies.

7.3.4 Bomb #4: A Lack of Business and Financial Discipline

There are a few business rules of thumb I've learned over the years. The first of these is to know the source of your revenues. I've seen many folks get involved in the great eyeball race without the slightest inkling regarding how, exactly, they are going to reel in revenues.

Steve Case understood that AOL's revenues would come primarily from online advertising and secondarily from subscriptions. Having a revenue model in which both subscriptions and advertising contribute to the bottom line can often spell success for dot.coms. This is the traditional media industry formula: subscriptions, subsidized by advertising. This approach has stood the test of time since the early days of newspapers and magazines.

However, it is dastardly difficult for firms on the Internet to get consumers into the habit of paying for subscriptions. Online and wireless service providers have trained us to pay for their services, but, beyond paying for the connection itself, consumers are very reticent to pay for anything else. Without an audience or audience demographics, it's very difficult to get advertisers to pay.

Therefore, many of the dot.bombs held on to a faint hope that they could get some advertising revenue, without having the slightest thought about who would be buying this advertising space on their sites. The lesson to be learned here is know from whence your revenues will come before you go to all the expense of taking your business to the Internet. Many of the traditional publishing companies have made a nice transition to the Internet and have brought their advertisers along with them because they know their audiences well.

7.3.5 Bomb #5: A Failure to Prove the Viability of Your Cost Structure

For the most part, I believe that, if your firm has $3 million in revenues and you still aren't profitable, the odds are you'll never be profitable, especially with startups. First they need to prove out their revenue models and cost structures and then get things sized in a way that they can deliver profit, early and often. This takes a steadfast discipline from Day One. There are a lot of companies in the dot.bomb bone yard that just didn't have the discipline to tighten their own belts in order to keep their businesses viable. They had too many fancy offices, fancy cars, fancy perks, and not enough raw business sense. Most seem to have no concept that they were living off investors' money and that they had a fiduciary duty to put the business interests of their investors ahead of immediate enhancements to their personal lifestyles. Of course, some of the investors showed a surprising lack of judgment by all at once dumping big buckets of money at the doorsteps of the dot.bombs.

7.3.6 Bomb #6: Dawdle Mania

A lot of dot.coms became dot.bombs because they were too slow in launching their sites and spent tons of time and money just preparing them. Companies in the hot dot.com era were spending a year or two working on their launch strategies, and, by the time they finally brought their businesses to the Internet, customers no longer had an interest in what they had to sell.

Conversely, if you look at some of the most successful companies on the Internet, you'll notice that they got out there early and evolved their sites as rapidly as they could in order to add additional value. There's just no substitute for getting the experience with the user community early on, at a low cost, and then building on that value going forward.

That sort of development model is very foreign to the average company. Yahoo! was one company that was extraordinarily good at getting out there early and then enhancing its services after it had the initial technology breakthrough. Even today, Yahoo! is evolving on a daily basis. No dawdling is going on within its doors.

7.3.7 Bomb #7: A Failure to Communicate

The lesson to be learned here is that it is critical to articulate every step of the customer relationship process before you take your business to the Internet. Even today, I see so many retailing Web sites that are poorly instrumented from a customer interface point of view.

Of course, from Day One, Amazon knew that its relationship with its customers was central to its success, and, because of this, Amazon erred on the side of overcommunicating with its customers, rather than undercommunicating. Overall, Amazon has found a good balance between positive communication and intrusive communication. It's done a pretty good job of tracking its active users and communicating with them at appropriate times. If you're not an active buyer on its site, it's unlikely that you'll be receiving a lot of unsolicited messages from Amazon. The key to these communications activities has been to make them personal and relevant to the customer.

7.4 The Secrets to Dot.Com Success

For those considering taking their business to the Internet, I'd like to offer these secrets to success:

- Define your revenue model up front.
- Develop a compelling set of value propositions and enhance it over time.
- Create a scaleable architecture.
- Don't spend too much on technology too early.
- Get things up fast and develop them with real customers.
- Pay close attention to physical logistics.
- Communicate wisely with your customers by doing such things as immediately acknowledging their online orders and the shipping status of those orders.
- Develop an early sense of profit discipline.

There's no guarantee that you'll become rich beyond your dreams by following these steps, but you certainly will have a better chance of positioning yourself on the fast track to profit.

7.5 Online Purchasing Purgatory

Before you jump into the dot.com world, I'd like to share with you one of my recent online retail experiences that happened to be particularly horrible. I hopped on the Internet and purchased a small widget. After I officially placed my order, I received absolutely no email confirmation that my order had been received. Was it received? I really needed this widget.

I thought about calling the company on its 1-800 number, but there was no such number posted on its Web site. Somehow I just knew my order was in trouble. Nevertheless, I decided, against my better judgment, to have faith that my widget would soon be winging its way to my Boise home.

I waited a week or two, and, to my surprise, my package showed up at my front door. Unfortunately, the company had shipped the wrong product. Good grief! Therefore, again, I needed to call the company. This time, I found a telephone number in the collateral pieces that were included with the incorrect product they sent to me, but, naturally, it wasn't even a toll-free number. I called the number and, much to my dismay, I ended up in a seemingly endless series of expensive telephone queues. This was such a big headache for such a little widget.

It makes a person wonder: What is wrong with these online companies?

For one thing, so many of these companies just haven't refined their own internal systems. Unless you're going to follow through by tuning up your own internal systems, your customers are going to have a bad experience. I can almost guarantee that. You can't just bolt something on to the front end of your Web site and expect the situation to be miraculously rectified.

I find a surprising number of online retailers that don't even bother to add anything onto the frontend of their sites. They just take the simplest commerce engine available, with absolutely no regard to the customer experience, and then they just start taking orders. Then, someone, somewhere, manually enters these orders, and, before you know it, orders are falling into a black hole with no visibility or communication with the customer.

It's a prescription for online purchasing purgatory. It's also the best way to ensure that you have both unhappy customers and customers who never return to your site again.

7.6 Online Purchasing Nirvana

A heavenly online purchasing experience begins with making your products easy to find online. So many companies just throw their catalogs online without any regard for the unique attributes of this medium. Beware. Most printed catalogs are not necessarily organized in a way that consumers will find easy to navigate if the catalogs are just thrown online without any redesign. It takes a fair amount of research into what your customers would find of interest and then a sharp Web designer to present your merchandise in an appealing way.

One of the real strengths of the Internet is that it allows consumers to dive more deeply into product features and function. I have found so many online retailers who don't take advantage of this feature and simply don't bother to link their products to additional information and content that they or their suppliers might have.

My recommendation is to just take your site to the next level by offering content linkages. You'll find this endeavor to be extremely valuable to your customers and to your ultimate bottom line.

Next, make the online experience heavenly for your customers by making the online ordering process incredibly simple and easy. Make it easy for your customers to get in and out of their shopping baskets. Above all, make it easy for them to keep adding items to their baskets.

Give your customers the chance to choose their preferred method of shipment. Some will want expedited service and will be willing to pay a premium for this service. Others will be completely satisfied with less expensive ground transportation. Whatever your customers choose, be sure to provide delivery date estimates, and, when available, hot link the FedEx, UPS, and U.S. Postal Service tracking numbers so that your customers can follow their orders from your door to theirs, with just a click of the mouse. Remember, all of these services are going to be downright difficult to provide if you are still using manual processes. With just a small financial investment in technology, these processes become a piece of cake.

You can buy yourself bushels of goodwill by providing an immediate acknowledgment of every order placed. Do this through an instant email message, which includes confirmation that the order has indeed been placed and that the credit card has been charged. Also include a status update on the items to be shipped. Trust me and automate this process.

I find so many companies that just haphazardly bolt these processes onto their frontends without automating their internal systems. These companies don't realize that their performance as a supplier is incredibly visible to their customers on the Internet. Believe me, those early customer experiences really do determine whether customers will come back to those sites in the future.

Remember, the customer experience does not end when you ship your product. The returns process generally has received poor attention. However, as unglamorous as this process is, it can have a startling impact on your company's profit picture. Keep in mind that the more times your product is touched means the more likely it is to arrive damaged. Therefore, consider shipping your products with preprinted return labels and enough packing material to cushion its journey from, and if needed, back to your warehouse.

7.7 Busy Signals

Let's face it. If you haven't figured out a way to make your business work in the physical world, just putting your business online isn't going to make it work either.

Here's the good news, however...

A number of industries out there have been able to serve various customer markets of under a million people and make some impressive amounts of money while doing so. These industries have done a superb job of exploiting the world's best Internet technologies in order to run their online businesses in an impressive, cost-effective manner.

For the wise and business savvy among us, opportunity abounds in this arena, and I think we've barely scratched the surface. I see a lot of promising opportunities ahead for those who choose to bring their business to the Internet. It's hard to predict the future with rock-solid accuracy, but I believe the outlook is quite bright.

Back in 1915, although ever so busy with the telephone and his other inventions, Alexander Graham Bell nevertheless took a moment to ponder the future. He noted, "The possibilities of further achievement by the use of electricity are inconceivable. Men can do nearly everything else by electricity already, and I can imagine them with coils of wire about their heads coming together for communication of thought by induction."

I wonder if Mr. Bell is looking down upon us today and thinking that gigabytes and megapixels are every bit as cool as coils of wires about people's heads.

CHAPTER   8

Insider Secrets Revealed

In a moment, I'm going to share some very powerful insider secrets that I've discovered during my career. These secrets, after they are revealed, will enable you to bypass all sorts of business roadblocks and will allow you, instead, to take the fast track to profit.

However, just in case *my* insider secrets don't do the trick for you, I thought I'd throw in a couple of *bonus* secrets from other, perhaps more worldly, insiders who are really in the know.

Interested? Well, then, how would you like to know how to marry a millionaire and how to find the fountain of youth?

Yes, I thought that would catch your attention!

The first *bonus* insider secret that I'd like to share with you comes from the 1953 Twentieth Century-Fox movie, *How to Marry a Millionaire.* This insider secret comes from none other than the beautiful, but terribly myopic, gold digger, Marilyn Monroe, who shared with her costars, Betty Grable and Lauren Bacall, her favorite bit of insider advice regarding how to marry a millionaire. What was her secret?

Lose the glasses, because Ms. Monroe said, "Men aren't attentive to girls who wear glasses."

OK. Perhaps this isn't the *best* insider secret in the world. (I say that as I'm lovingly glancing across the room at my spectacled bride, and best friend, of 30 years.)

Hmmm. Let's instead consider a second, tried-and-true, bonus insider secret for achieving the elusive fountain of youth. Let's go to the Number One source on the topic: Dick Clark. Believe it or not, Dick Clark was born on November 30, 1929. Amazing, isn't it? This septuagenarian has the sparkle and spring of a 30-year-old.

The New York Post writer, Dan Aquilante, recently interviewed Mr. Clark about his secret for finding the fountain of youth. Mr. Aquilante said this about "Mr. New Year's Eve" in his December 28, 2001 article: "Dick Clark, America's perennial teenager, says staying young is a snap. 'It's easy,' the 72-year-old told *The Post*. 'I've been a part of the American music scene for more than 50 years. When you grow up with music like I did, and all the people around you are young, you maintain the attitude.'" When it comes to great insider secrets, you can really dance to that tune.

Now, let's swing over to some insider secrets that can pave your way to the fast track to profit.

8.1 Insider Secret #1: Linking People and Processes

The Internet is a much more flexible kind of technology than anyone originally thought it would be. In the past, various waves of information technology had required data to be highly structured in order to link it into some sort of a coherent business process. What you get with the Internet is the amazing ability to link structured and unstructured data together with a user interface that lets you provide a lot of contextual information. Previously, that was not possible. This is truly a remarkable revolution.

The Internet has provided company after company with breakthrough methods for providing enormously helpful and efficient business environments within which their employees can work. In addition, Internet technologies have opened up millions of opportunities for automating and streamlining business processes that were previously isolated and incoherent.

For example, up until about 1996, Microsoft steadfastly resisted the Internet. Now, that's an insider secret you might not have known. Then, Microsoft realized that the Internet was real and that the Internet was passing it by. It was enough of a psychological jolt to prompt Microsoft to undertake radical initiatives to change the way it was doing business.

Microsoft started by bringing in Web server architecture into its product family. Then, Microsoft brought in its own browser, which it began delivering as part of the desktop environment. Of course, that was the beginning of the latest round of antitrust problems the company was going to encounter. Nevertheless, these aggressive moves into the world of Internet technology suddenly gave Microsoft employees the tools that they needed to automate just about every internal business process around this new set of Web paradigms.

This transformation at Microsoft had two big benefits. First of all, it caused everybody at the company to think about the potential of the Internet. Second, Microsoft was able to make a lot more business progress toward automating its internal operations.

All of this happened at a time when the Microsoft business portfolio was expanding dramatically. The Internet gave Microsoft the ability to scale up its business more profitably. Microsoft was able to maintain an impressive cost structure throughout the massive growth it was undergoing in terms of the size and scope of its business.

Most other companies haven't exploited Internet technologies with such aplomb. Some companies have embraced the religion of the Internet and started automating one process after another. The problem many have faced, however, is that, after one process is automated, it exposes the current gaps in the rest of these companies' business processes—gaps that wouldn't have been exposed before.

The danger is that it's so easy to automate individual pieces of the puzzle that sometimes companies don't take the time to step back and examine all of their processes end to end. If you're not careful, you might cast in concrete a set of older business processes that really could be more radically transformed by a second or third order of transformation, following up on the initial transformation. Too many companies dig in and only take the first step of automation, for which they typically get a huge short-term payback. Then they say, "Well, that's done," and they forget that this must be an evolutionary process.

The best secret I've discovered in this regard is that enormous benefits can be realized if you immediately go back the moment you finish the first round of automation and reinvest in a second round of automation in order to make your underlying processes even more efficient. This becomes easier the second time around because, during your first round of automation, you'll have learned much about your entire corporate business structure. Reinvest that knowledge in a second round of automation, and you will not believe the benefits you will reap. Both the developers and your business process leaders will know how to do things much better after the first automation effort, yet most companies throw away that expensive, hard-earned knowledge by failing to follow through on the initial breakthrough.

By using Internet technologies to link people and processes, you will empower people to make decisions at a level closer to where the decisions actually have an impact. In the long run, this will save your company a lot of time, effort, and money. You'll end up with a decentralized organizational design, featuring flatter organizational structures. This will help your organization become much more nimble, which is a tremendous advantage in today's fast-moving world.

In addition, as you flatten your organization, you'll need fewer people to handle the coordination function of your business. Thus, your management chains get flatter, along with their associated bureaucracies. This will allow your business to be much more efficient and more responsive to customers and opportunities.

These things won't happen by accident. You'll have to jump in there and make sure your team doesn't fall into a trap that so many companies have experienced. Typically, these companies will automate a certain process while still keeping their current management structure in place. They don't recognize that the underlying processes have shifted in some fashion and that there will be new opportunities for further shifts in the underlying processes of the organization.

An example of a company that has not fallen into this trap is Cisco. It has been relentless in the way that it has eliminated quite a few layers of management as its processes have become automated. Cisco has been able to do this while growing into a much more complex company with lots of diverse product lines.

What is Cisco's secret? The company has done an excellent job of automating and standardizing its processes, allowing it to scale much more rapidly into adjacent businesses. By the way, almost the first thing that Cisco does when it buys a new business is to go in and change the IT infrastructure of that business so that its processes are more standardized, more visible, and more empowering to the employees.

As you know, I was an executive at IBM for many years. Like Cisco, IBM has done a phenomenal job of automating and standardizing its processes. When IBM acquired Lotus, the Lotus Notes product was essentially a standalone product. IBM began to reap real benefits when it created the Domino product, which made it incredibly easy to move content to and from the Web.

That gave IBM the ability to manipulate contextual information around its business processes with the Lotus Notes architecture. IBM was able to automate many of its business processes fairly quickly in a highly structured kind of environment. This process was radically deployed throughout IBM—almost overnight—because of the powerful Domino architecture the company put in place.

In my current role as chief technology officer for HP's Printing and Imaging business, I've been able to be a part of the major reengineering HP has done to link its people to its processes. HP deployed an employee portal in 2000, which initially had a bit of trouble getting off the ground, but, after a few challenges were overcome, it took off like a rocket. We were all pretty shocked at how quickly the HP employee portal took hold. HP's vision was to have a single place employees could go to in order to do just about anything they wanted to do. This portal was to have standard employee forms and approval mechanisms, along with a full set of management tools.

By the launching the HP employee portal, we were able to integrate all of these formerly discrete processes and presentations into a single, coherent Web presence. Before we launched the HP employee portal, we had to log onto 10 or 15 different systems while searching for a desired form. Today, we just do a single login, and all the tools we need for both employee and management functions are right at our fingertips. No further login or authentication is needed. It's brilliant, it's simple, and it's visually attractive.

Of course, in order to architect and launch our employee portal, we had to look underneath our own covers and come face to face with a lot of gaps and holes in our internal processes. It wasn't the most pleasant experience, but it certainly was an eye-opener. It also helped emphasize for us the importance of getting the portal up and running.

The HP employee portal has enabled us to put a lot of contextual information right online. There also has been a massive amount of content that we've created in order to have the information our employees need, whenever and wherever they need it. In addition, the user interface we've created for the portal is clean and clear, making the whole process of searching for just the right tool quite intuitive. Now that we have the HP employee portal, it's tough to imagine how we ever got by without it.

I wish someone would come up with an equally ingenious solution to the problem I have in my private life, with all of the different remote control units with which I have to contend. You'd think that someone could develop a true universal remote control unit. A single button would open my garage door. Another button would help me locate one of the several wireless phones I have lying around my house, and, for goodness sake, the unit truly would be able to operate my TV and my CD player, along with my DVD machine and my VCR.

I know there are products that claim they can control every gizmo and gadget in your home, but they don't. Therefore, my wife has a collection of four remote controls that she keeps in a basket by our bed. It's ridiculous, and we're reminded of this every night.

Mark my words: Someday soon, someone is going to make a bundle of money by creating the perfect universal remote. All of our devices will have their own Web addresses, and everything we own will have the potential for being practically interoperable.

Someday soon, someone is going to take our new Internet architecture, including its philosophies and design points, and figure out a way to drive it through other parts of our economy, including our personal environments.

Meanwhile, one of the surefire ways you can lead your company to the fast track to profit is to begin the necessary steps to link your people to your processes. Unfortunately, there really is no cheap and easy way to do this.

How should you begin? You'll have to start by taking a very hard look at your core business processes and applying the right enabling tools to either your existing IT infrastructure or to a new IT infrastructure that can easily handle these new tools. Remember, you'll need to work in an Internet paradigm to reap the greatest results from your efforts, and the best way of doing that is to use some sort of Java process. Soon, .NET also will probably work. After you've done that basic enabling, you'll want to start looking across all of your business practices to find out where gaps and seams exist that could be eliminated through automation.

You'll find the Web really shines, particularly where structured data meets unstructured data. However, for a real kick-start, begin with all the easy pickings: the business processes that are very structured and replicable. You'll find that automating these will be fast and easy. Then, work on all of the unstructured information and irregular kinds of activities that people within your company do on a regular basis. This part of the job will not be as easy, but the rewards will be significant.

In creating our own HP employee portal, we had some early assistance from Yahoo! However, there was just so much that it could do with our user interface requirements, and, from there, HP had to do the rest. After all, no one could possibly understand the depth and breadth of our business processes better than our own people. At the end of the day, we quickly discovered that it was more about making those business processes meet individuals than it was about making sure we had the 20 most popular hit sites on our portal home page. Basically, we really ran out of runway fairly early with Yahoo!

When attacking the challenge of linking your people to your processes, you'll either need to have your own internal IT team fully engaged on this project, or you'll have to bring in a very solid IT professional services company to help you. Experience tells me that more and more companies have discovered that creating this new Internet environment for linking people and processes is very challenging, and typically requires the help of outside companies.

Of course, the ultimate benefits of doing this work will be incredible. With a new streamlined set of business processes, you'll instantly have a more productive and pleasant employee experience. Your employees will also be more empowered, allowing them to have fast and easy access to enough contextual information to make decisions closer to the customer. They'll also be able to make decisions closer to your supply chains.

In summary, I recommend you link people and processes by taking the following steps:

- Exploit the power of the Internet by automating as many of your internal processes as possible.

- Immediately after your first round of automation, go back and reinvest in a second round of automation in order to further streamline your processes.
- Standardize your processes with those of your business partners.
- Raise the visibility of these newly automated processes so your employees will feel immediately empowered to begin making decisions closer to the customer.
- Continuously look for gaps and seams that could be eliminated through further automation.
- Make sure you have a first-rate IT team dedicated to linking your people and processes.
- Ensure that you also change management mindsets, culture, and structure so that old patterns don't subvert the breakthroughs.

8.2 Insider Secret #2: Linking Electronic and Physical Universes

As I mentioned earlier, Cisco did an incredible job of automating every aspect of the internal side of its business. The folks at Cisco then discovered that, much to their horror, they had neglected to automate their supply chain to the extent that they should have. Because Cisco's supply chain was so heavily outsourced and leveraged, the company found itself vulnerable to the downshift in the economy. It got stuck with too much inventory, work in progress, and a variety of other anchors, including inventory out in the channel that it didn't realize it had. To put it concisely, Cisco got bombarded with problems, all related to its supply and distribution chains.

The same precarious situation engulfed the folks at Amazon, despite the fact that they had done such a glorious job of building their online presence. Of course, they were lucky that they had a fairly automated book warehouse operation upon which they had built their original business. However, as they started to expand their product lines, they needed to raise their overall profit structure by increasing average transactions, and, frankly, they had a tough time pulling all the supply chain logistics together to form a more comprehensive online retailing experience.

Keep in mind that, in any organization, you have physical boundaries where your organization meets the interface with your customers or suppliers. Oftentimes, this intersection happens on paper.

Today, more than half of the households in the United States have Internet access, with many fewer subscribing to online billing services. Therefore, at some stage, your business will likely have to convert electronic ordering information received at the boundaries of your business into a paper format. This paper will then have to fit into existing physical information flows or existing product flows, or both, in some fashion. As you might imagine, when you move from the electronic universe into the physical universe, all sorts of mistakes can happen.

One company, however, that has done a stellar job of moving between the electronic universe and the physical universe is Wal-Mart. It has done an incredible job of automating every aspect of its supply chain. Wal-Mart is widely hailed as one of the most efficient companies in the world at doing this.

I started talking to Dayton Hudson, the owner of Target, about the Internet back in the mid-1990s. At that time, the company was not particularly interested in using the Internet to serve customers, but it was very intrigued about using it to improve its supply chain. As you may know, Dayton Hudson has tried to position Target as an upscale discount store. Therefore, it has been imperative that Dayton Hudson be able to acquire a higher grade of merchandise than its competitors in order to differentiate itself in the marketplace. Dayton Hudson has been able to achieve this, in part, because of its investment in automating its supply chain. I really admire its relentless focus in this regard, and its efforts have certainly paid off.

Kmart, on the other hand, is now involved in bankruptcy proceedings partially because it failed to focus on improving its supply chain. Kmart had one heck of a hard time delivering hot products when they came out in the marketplace. It either underbought or couldn't respond fast enough to hot products. Therefore, Kmart got stuck with more products in inventory than it really needed, and the products it had weren't very hot. As you know, inventory management in a low margin, high turnover business is critical, and Kmart just was not up to this challenge.

If you look at retailing, in particular, you'll find that most retail operations are highly automated at the point of sale. There has been a massive investment in information technology in this industry so that, when items are individually scanned, the information can be examined, interpreted, and acted upon by the inventory team.

The questions you must ask, however, are have you automated *every* step of that process so you really have the kind of visibility you should? Do you have the right people and processes in place to pay attention to that data and make your supply chain almost hair-triggered? If you are involved in any kind of retail business or if you are a part of the retail delivery chain, it's very important that you ask these questions.

For small and medium businesses, the odds are pretty high that you're part of somebody else's supply chain. The majority of these businesses are quite often supplying specific components or very narrow value propositions, increasing the likelihood that they truly are, indeed, part of somebody else's supply chain. The important thing to remember in these cases is that it's imperative to have your business and your IT systems using Internet technology so that these systems can readily link to your customers and your supply chain partners.

One of the great challenges for small and medium businesses is to learn to leverage the services of other companies, particularly in the area of inventory management. Believe me. I've seen a lot of small and medium businesses get hung up on inventory problems.

At HP, we've just finished going through a fairly detailed examination of our supply chain issues. As a result, we have basically outsourced a fair amount of our parts business to UPS. We now stock our parts at the UPS depot, as opposed to stocking them in our own facilities. Because UPS is actually delivering our products, we now have fewer order and delivery problems, and our products are delivered faster. To top it off, our overall costs in this area have been dramatically reduced.

I think small and medium-sized businesses, to a large extent, simply have not thought through their value delivery chains. With companies out there like UPS, these small and medium businesses have a real opportunity to access the same world-class logistics capabilities that larger companies, like HP, have accessed. It's a golden opportunity just waiting to be grabbed.

Increasingly, there are new companies that just specialize in the logistics part of the delivery chain. A number of very large contract manufacturing consortiums can actually handle a lot more manufacturing needs than many small and medium-sized businesses realize.

During the past four or five years, the Internet has allowed exceptional collaborative design opportunities, along with impressive just-in-time delivery options. Unfortunately, a lot of small and medium-sized businesses are simply unaware of these available resources, especially those businesses that are located in remote areas. Many of these companies might actually be able to outsource a fair amount of their design work to companies located nearer to major transportation hubs without physically having any employees in the area of these hubs.

Opportunity is knocking. Are you listening? If not, I urge you to stop, look, and follow these steps in order to better link your electronic and physical universes:

- Automate as many steps of as many processes as practical, given the size and nature of your business, so that critical information gets the visibility it needs.
- Make sure you have the right people and processes in place that can pay attention to incoming data.
- Automate your supply chain so that it is almost hair-triggered.
- Standardize on Internet technology so your business and your IT systems can link to whoever your customers or your supply chain partners happen to be.

8.3 Insider Secret #3: Building and Sustaining Value Delivery Relationships and Partnerships

As you design your business processes, it is critical that you think about how these process might be linked together with other companies or organizations in delivering the ultimate value to your customers. Remember, the customers see very little of what happens between the time they place the order and when the order is received. That makes it all the more important that your company develop efficient and harmonious relationships with your value delivery partners.

Maybe your company is a supplier to a large cataloging operation like Amazon. How do you ensure that the customer gets the latest information on your product? One way to do that is for you to upload files on your products directly to Amazon. The other way you can deliver that information to the customer is by having a hot link back into your own site where the customer can get the most up-to-date information available. Of course, if you take this path, you'll also have to provide an absolutely seamless transition back into

Amazon (or whatever large cataloging operation you're linked into) so that the purchase can actually occur. Making this happen can be very complex, and, if any portion of the process is broken, the customer is likely to have a fairly sad and bad experience.

My recommendation to you is to look ever so closely at every angle of your business from the customer's point of view. Consider everything your customer is likely to see during the process of getting information about your product and during the process of actually buying your product.

Think about the underlying technology architecture you are using and how your information is delivered. Consider the purchase experience and look for ways to solidify your linkages in a more meaningful and substantive sort of way.

You could, for example, work with a company like Amazon and actually edit your content on its site, as opposed to hosting your own site and having a link go across. You also could use the same hosting vendor that one of your major partners uses so that any failures are contained in the network infrastructure of the hosting vendor, as opposed to being contained in more unreliable links.

Remember that there's just no substitute for looking at your underlying technology delivery infrastructure. Again, start with the customer experience. Examine it inside and out. Then, think through your IT delivery infrastructure by having some solid professional people examine your architecture. These folks will look for opportunities to provide better delivery at a better cost.

Back in my old law school days, one of my professors had been part of a very successful law practice. One of his insider tips for how to run a good law firm was to place an anonymous call to your own office every so often to see how things look to your clients. It is unbelievable how many bad telephone systems, receptionists, and terrible Web sites are out there. I honestly believe that more than 90 percent of the Web sites are disasters waiting to happen, and the majority of these disasters happen about the time your customer wants to buy something from you.

Next, take a hard look at your linkages for physical logistics. Then, see if there's an opportunity to leverage one of the major parties, such as UPS, in your delivery chain. Keep in mind that there is just no substitute for the kind of deep, step-by-step, process-by-process look at how to improve both the response time and the efficiency and effectiveness of your cross-organizational boundary issues.

In summary, consider the following:

- Look at every angle of your business from your customer's point of view.
- Consider your underlying technology architecture, and, if it's not delivering the kind of results you expect, bring in the IT experts.
- Explore ways to solidify your linkages into the purchasing experience.
- Tap into first-rate linkages for physical logistics.

8.4 Insider Secret #4: Strengthening the Relationship with Your Customers

The best secret that I can pass along to you in this category is to personalize the relationship with your customers whenever possible. Truly get to know your customer in a high-touch way, if possible. If your Web site can help you, great, but you can't develop a customer-centered discipline in your IT environment if you don't know what your customer needs.

Most companies have found that they really haven't done a good job of integrating all of the places and processes their customers touch. At HP, for example, the first time we typically touch our end customers is when they send us a warranty card. For the most part, our products flow through channels, so we don't see the customers until they have problems with our products or when they send in a warranty card. For a while, we hadn't integrated this incoming information particularly well, but, believe me, this has now become a priority at HP.

A lot of HP resources are now dedicated toward pulling together a unified architecture and linking all of our interactions with customers. This isn't done in a snooping sort of way, but rather it's done to simplify our interactions with our customers.

For example, if you, as a customer, were to place several individual orders with one of your favorite companies, over a period of several months, you wouldn't want to have to give the company your address and telephone number each time you placed a new order. Most customers appreciate the fact that their favorite companies have this information instantly accessible. Some companies also ask only for the last four numbers of the credit cards of repeat customers. Some folks are a bit sensitive about this, while others appreciate the streamlined approach to ordering that this enables.

Let's face it, as technology permeates throughout so many facets of our lives, it's not always easy to remember all of the PIN numbers and pass codes that are required when we purchase products.

Therefore, as you look at your own company's relationship with your customers, consider the benefits of allowing your customers to create their own, easy-to-remember identities online, including their own PIN numbers and pass codes. Companies arrogant enough to choose PIN numbers for their customers are asking for trouble. When ordering online, if you cannot access your shopping cart because you can't remember the arbitrary PIN number the company assigned to you, you may very well just log off in frustration. Therefore, make things as simple and pleasant as you can for your customers.

Also, consider the many benefits of data mining. We haven't quite reached the stage where every single product can be customized. It's easier, for example, to produce thousands of pants with a 36-inch waist than to make one for a customer with a 35 and 3/4-inch waist and another for a different customer with a 36 and 1/4-inch waist, and so on.

However, we have reached the point where we can break our customers into coherent groups and produce products that are at least more personalized from their point of view. Data mining can provide enormous insight into your customers' buying patterns and preferences and can offer helpful insights that can allow you to create more personalized experiences for your customers.

Even small or medium-sized businesses still need some way to characterize their customers. Luckily, a number of excellent online tools will help you structure your Web site so you can understand the pattern of activity that characterizes each customer visit to your site. The good news is that these tools are very affordable, even for the smallest of businesses. These tools won't be able to define customer intent or context clearly, but they will provide some valuable information nevertheless.

A plethora of valuable information is just waiting to be accessed from your Web site. I highly recommend that you use the available tools to capture this customer information because it will provide your business with incredible knowledge about your customers' needs, wants, and interests. And you know what they say about knowledge...

Ask your Web developer to suggest the best set of tools to use in conjunction with your particular Web site. If I were you, I'd do this today. If you aren't studying your customers' online clicking patterns, you're passing up one of the most important sources of market intelligence out there.

In the old days, we used to spend a fortune on user interface design. This included customer usability research, where we looked at the ways users interacted with software through one-way mirrors. With Internet technology, we can monitor the way customers navigate information and functions on the Web site. In addition, because most of the Web site is server, rather than client driven, you can innovate the user interaction "on the fly." The way that most Web sites are designed, it is obvious that these advanced tools are not in widespread use.

To a certain extent, the longer you can keep your customers on your site by providing interesting and useful content means the better your chances are that your customers will buy something from your company. You do, however, have to pay special attention to the actual purchasing process. One study indicated that fewer than 20 percent of items placed in online shopping carts are actually purchased. One of the major reasons is that the follow-on interaction with the customer is so confusing that the customer gets frustrated and leaves the site. Remember, on the Internet, all it takes is a single mouse click, and the customer is gone.

Another problem is that the process of purchasing takes so long that the customer loses interest. A good Web site continues marketing the item through the entire purchase process. Posting small pictures or listing product advantages on the shopping cart list is a powerful tool used by the best online retailers. Subtlety works well here. Some folks think that the Amazon process of suggesting other related purchases may actually distract customers from concluding the original purchase.

Another place people get lost on Web sites is in the shopping cart function itself. Most online shopping experiences place items in a shipping cart and then ask if the customer wants to check out or do more shopping. In almost all cases, if the customer wants to continue shopping, the customer is redirected to the company's home page, rather than to the last place they were visiting when they put the item into the shopping cart.

Again, even some basic instrumentation of the Web site would easily identify where in the shopping and buying process you are losing your customers. This can be some of the best work you ever do. It is also not a bad idea to compare your site to those of your competitors. If the rest of the industry seems to be sleepy in this regard, you might have a huge opportunity that can be quickly exploited. Just remember that you have to invest in conventional customer communication to draw customers to your site.

That is why it is critical to analyze your the basic instrumentation so that you can understand where your customers are getting lost. You may well discover that a huge number of customers have put items from your site into their shopping carts, only to have their transactions crash. Perhaps your customers are bailing out of your site because you are making it so difficult for them to complete their orders.

Have you made it impossibly cumbersome for your customers to give you their money? For example, do you ask your customers to fill out an entire page of personal information only to find that, when they click Submit, the whole page comes back to them with an admonishment that they neglected to fill in a certain field? Why dump the entire page back in your customers' laps? Wouldn't it be much nicer if your site were set up so that only incomplete fields reappeared? Remember, if you make your customers jump through too many hoops, it's likely that the final hoop through which they jump takes them directly from your site to your competitor's.

Another challenge is that the search functions for the online catalogs are essentially useless. This is often because the catalog is stored in some sort of structured database, and the Web site developers usually are lazy and use standard structured database query mechanisms. Much more powerful search tools are available, but, as Yahoo! proved, often the most helpful search information is to use human beings to structure the information into useful categories.

Amazon has done a fantastic job of eliminating the hoops on its site. For repeat customers, it offers true, one-click ordering. This is a vast improvement over most retail sites on the Internet today. The Amazon folks really worked hard on this architecture. The key to creating the final interface was the relentless attention that the Amazon team paid to its customers' buying and surfing habits.

For those who prefer to peruse your site, I recommend that you provide good navigational guidance during both the investigation and purchase processes.

Remember, though, that your work does not end when the sale is closed. Much goodwill can be gained by providing positive communication to your customers from this point forward. An automatic confirmation should be emailed to each customer as soon as an order is placed. Soon thereafter, you should email your customers their tracking numbers with hot links to UPS, FedEx, or other shippers' sites so that they know exactly when to expect their packages to arrive. Of course, in order to swing this in a flawless fashion, you'll need world-class integration of your Web site and your email system.

Therefore, in conclusion, I recommend that you strengthen the relationship with your customers by taking the following steps:

- Make sure your search function is easy and useful.
- Provide navigational guidance on your site.
- Make the ordering process simple and pleasant.
- Personalize your customer relationship whenever possible.
- Create a unified IT infrastructure that links all of your interactions with your customers.
- Allow your customers to create their own identities on your site.
- Study your customers' clicking behavior and analyze ways in which their experiences on your site can be streamlined.
- Provide positive communication and feedback to your customers so that they know exactly where they are in the buying process.
- Provide instant confirmation numbers after orders have been placed.
- Provide tracking numbers with hot links so that your customers can follow their purchases through actual delivery to their front doors.

I urge you to exploit these insider secrets to your greatest advantage. You'll find that, in doing so, you'll be able to provide more value to your customers while empowering your employees to make decisions in a more timely and efficient fashion.

You know the secrets. Now, picture yourself on the fast track to profit.

Famed writer and poet Dorothy Parker did just that, as she surmised, "I don't know much about being a millionaire, but I'll bet I'd be a darling at it."

Driving the Internet: Step-by-Step Owner's Manual

$\mathbf{H}$ave you ever noticed how solving one problem can create an entirely new one? Well, here's a little story that happened to me back in the 1980s that illustrates this point perfectly.

I knew a fellow then, Peter Phillips, who was an economist at the University of Utah. One day Peter and I were talking about our theories regarding bottlenecks in technology development. It was then that he told me the following story about his experiences in the canneries in Northern California. I can think of no better way to illustrate the bottleneck theory.

You see, when Peter was a young man, he worked in the canneries, canning tomatoes. This was an especially popular job for young people who were putting themselves through school or raising a family.

Anyway, as you may know, the canning industry has a long history of developing new machines for various stages of the canning process. First, in order to meet a growing market demand for tomatoes, the industry developed lightning-fast canners. However, it then had a new problem on its hands. How could it feed the fast canners *fast enough* to match the rate of the new canning machines? Therefore, the industry developed the technology to drop the tomatoes into the cans at a pace that could keep up with conveyor belts delivering the cans.

That, unfortunately, created yet another new problem. Now the industry found that it couldn't get the tomatoes out of the field fast enough. It couldn't keep up with the new technology it had installed in the cannery to drop the food into the cans that were whizzing by at a breakneck pace on the conveyor belts. The industry then had to invent faster tomato-harvesting machines, which it proudly did.

Was the problem solved? Heck no!

The faster tomato-harvesting machines required that the tomatoes be harvested at a greener stage in their lifecycle. This was no problem, except for the fact that greener tomatoes, though curiously tangy, don't appeal to most people, which is putting it mildly.

OK. Scientists then had to go in and reengineer the actual tomatoes.

The point is that you must be prepared for this inevitability: When you fix one problem, you may be creating another. In other words, when you automate one process, you may just be moving your bottlenecks around.

That won't necessarily be a bad thing because, as you continuously reengineer and perfect your processes, you'll greatly increase your chances for enjoying the sweet taste of success.

How do you like them tomatoes?

9.1 Looking at Your Communications Infrastructure

Most companies develop a communications infrastructure on an incremental basis. The problem with this approach is that these companies end up with a crazy-quilt strategy characterized by a patchwork of communications technologies that don't interoperate particularly well. Moreover, they cost too much to operate and prevent the company from taking advantage of ongoing advances in communications and information technology.

Unless you look at your communications infrastructure at least every two or three years, I'm afraid you won't be reaping the kinds of efficiencies that can help drive profit through your organization. Remember that the technologies of the Internet are changing so dramatically—and so quickly—that benefits you never before dreamed possible can be attained with ease today.

I encourage you to undertake a periodic process of having current and prospective vendors rebid your WANs and telecommunications services so as to provide a first-class communications infrastructure. You'll be amazed at how economies of scale are continuing to drive down the cost of providing an outstanding communications infrastructure.

A classic example of how not to manage your communications infrastructure can be found with our U.S. government. In 1995, the federal government signed a five-year contract to procure long-distance services. Almost before the ink on the contract was dry, the government ended up with a five-year commitment to pay significantly more for its long-distance services than the prevailing market rates.

The point is that, in this day and age, if you don't look at your communications infrastructure every two or three years, you're likely going to be paying more than you need to and have a set of services that may hold your business back.

I'd also like to recommend that you have some frank and in-depth conversations with several telecommunications providers. If you can leverage a single telecommunications company's infrastructure, you'll quite often get a better rate by allowing them to backhaul through their network, rather than requiring them to match their network exactly to your physical locations.

In addition, it's critical that you look at your applications infrastructure. Quite often, if you just look at your telecommunications infrastructure independent of your applications, you might end up perpetuating two or three legacy networks, rather than sharing a more common network infrastructure. On the other hand, you might also pass up the opportunity to consolidate or reengineer applications if you don't look at the network infrastructure in parallel with the applications infrastructure. I highly recommend taking a look at your applications infrastructure at least every year or two in order to migrate your legacy applications into a more common network infrastructure.

You may have considered doing this two or three years ago and decided it was cost-prohibitive to change your application base. However, consider the fact that you might very well be continuing to spend money on a proprietary networking protocol or a proprietary network system that could be migrated much more easily.

Remember, this is something that SITA, which provides integrated telecommunications solutions for the air transportation industry, has done so well by staying on the cutting edge of technology and thereby taking costs out of its infrastructure. SITA takes advantage of every new wave of service deployments as soon as they're available. Occasionally, this has required some change to SITA's application base, but it has been more than worth the investment. SITA has been able to do this because of an extremely capable networking team and a great partnership between the applications team and the networking team.

Next, it is imperative that you consider scalability issues. Unfortunately, many companies have locked themselves into legacy leased-line services, which typically have fixed rates attached to them. These services provide speeds that range anywhere from 64 kilobits per second to somewhere between 1.5 and 45 megabits per second (for T1 lines and DS3 lines).

Increasingly, there are ways of buying capacity in a more flexible manner. These plans usually charge a set fee for a committed data rate. On top of that, additional capacity is available on demand, up to a burst data rate. This can give your company some flexibility in its headroom so that you don't have to buy the highest capacity pipe to use at all times. This new method of purchasing allows you to buy for your average capacity, not your peak capacity.

When your company needs additional capacity, you can purchase that temporary bandwidth just when you need it. By the way, that's one instance when the Internet can be critically important, especially during high-burst interludes associated with new product introductions. Another time when this will come in handy is when your company is experiencing a technical support problem, which generates increased demand on your communications infrastructure. Having the flexibility to alter your networking architecture is critical. Finally, in the case of systems or network failure, having burst capacity on your remaining lines, or to other data centers, can make the difference between staying online (and in business) or not.

When it comes to scalability issues, I recommend that you look at your internal network infrastructure, both in terms of the raw bandwidth you'll need in your network and the way your routing issues are handled. In order to do this, you'll need to examine closely the way your network topology is laid out.

One of the most rapidly developing areas of networking is wireless Local Area Network (LAN). This technology offers the advantage of flexibility in locating workstations and supports mobility in the marketplace environment. It is not, however, the answer to all networking problems.

Physical limitations of the site may make it hard to deploy and use. Security concerns may overrule its use in some business settings that require the utmost in privacy. Finally, it may not provide enough bandwidth for some applications and workgroups.

Look at your network infrastructure every year or two. You'll need to do this because routing, switching, and networking technologies change pretty radically every two or three years. If you're not keeping up with these radical changes, you'll find your own communications infrastructure falling into a state of imbalance.

Next, you must consider reliability issues as they relate to your communications infrastructure. Generally, the newer communications technologies hitting the marketplace are more reliable than the older ones. Part of the reason for this is that communications software has been radically simplified, enabling much higher reliability. In addition, these software applications are more often than not baked right into the firmware of the various network hardware systems, again improving the prospect for rock-solid reliability. As you may know, in most networks, the number one source of reliability problems is in the software, not the hardware, and the number two source of reliability problems is in the cabling.

Applications software failures continue to be problematic with Internet applications. This is because most Internet applications use multiple servers to deliver the application, and a failure in any of the application components may mean that the entire system is essentially unusable. By simplifying your software maintenance environment and looking at your overall reliability issues on an ongoing basis, you'll know if you have deployed the right technology or if it's time for an upgrade, consolidation, or retirement.

The way Internet applications are typically developed is not usually the way you want to deploy them for reliability or cost of operations. The strength of Internet applications is that they are fast to develop and modify. The danger is that, if you do not look at the way they are put together and operated on a regular basis, you probably are incurring higher operating costs than you should, and you most likely are operating on the brink of operational disaster.

The next area that you'll need to examine pertains to security. You'll need to ensure the physical security of your communications infrastructure. Make certain that the cable between your computer systems is private, and that nothing else is running on it, or that you have adequate technology for ensuring that unauthorized users cannot get access to the physical network infrastructure. Sooner or later, most computers end up being cross-linked. This can lead to security holes in your network operating systems and in the way applications are deployed.

After you ensure the physical security of your communications infrastructure, you'll need to ensure the security of your applications infrastructure.

A lot of small and medium-sized companies will develop a more casual style of operation while they have only a handful of employees working on various projects. However, as companies get larger, they run into problems pertaining to disgruntled, or, in some cases, mentally ill employees, or even saboteurs, who are paid by other companies to sabotage or compromise their network or their operations. Therefore, internal security regarding your applications becomes a very high priority and will help your company lessen its chances of becoming a target for hackers and other criminals.

If you are working with a hosting vendor, you and your vendor must consider the full spectrum of security issues. This is of the utmost importance because you may have private network linkages back into your enterprise data, and appropriate firewalls must be installed to protect your data.

Another thing to consider is the interoperability between your systems and those of your trading partners. Your network and its operations are only as secure as the weakest link. With so many companies linking vendors, suppliers, and so forth, it's no longer enough to look at only your own turf for potential problems. You have to look at your trading partners and perhaps even their trading partners. After all, we're all in this networked world together.

Again, as you know, there have been a number of notorious hacking incidents where people have broken into brand-name computer systems. The Federal Bureau of Investigations (FBI), for one, was hacked into, much to its surprise and horror. Hackers also have found a way to post pornography on several name-brand company sites.

Unfortunately, a large group of people in the world gets its jollies out of trying to destroy the brand name or the image of upstanding companies. Many of these people do this on a lark, or for a hobby, and some do it for more sinister reasons. Just be aware that this is an issue that you must consider, and, as such, it's important to invest the necessary resources to make certain that your communications infrastructure has a very secure underlying architecture.

To review, I urge you to follow this step-by-step examination of your communications infrastructure:

- Examine your entire communications infrastructure every two or three years.
- Periodically rebid the WAN links and telecommunications services to provide your company with a first-class communications infrastructure.
- Discuss your communications infrastructure needs with at least two of the major telecommunications providers.
- Examine your entire applications infrastructure at least every year or two, with a special emphasis on fast-developing Internet applications.
- Consider the various scalability issues related to your communications infrastructure.
- Consider purchasing bandwidth on a committed data rate plan; purchase temporary bandwidth only when your company needs a burst of capacity.
- Look at your routing and switching topologies and update them as necessary.
- Consider the various reliability issues related to your communications infrastructure.
- Simplify and automate your software maintenance environment. Change management and control are extremely important where fast development is an operational necessity.
- Look at your reliability issues on an ongoing basis.
- Consider the physical, logical, and access security of your communications infrastructure.
- Consider the security of your applications infrastructure.
- If you use a hosting vendor, ensure that security and operations plans are well developed and understood.
- Install firewalls wherever appropriate.

9.2 Focusing on People, Not Processes

As you drive your organization toward the fast track to profit, it is imperative that you focus on empowering your employees to make decisions close to your customers and business processes. Toward this end, you'll want to take a hard look at your organizational design and the technology you have put in place to support that design. You'll also want to take a closer look at your business processes. Ask yourself if they are primarily paper driven. If so, you must reevaluate areas that can be automated. Often, doing so will save your company a lot of time and a considerable amount of money. It also will provide the foundation for faster information collection, analysis, and decision making.

The best way to empower your employees is to give them the knowledge and the information they need to make good and timely decisions. Then you must provide them with the tools to implement those decisions quickly and effectively. Wherever possible, using technology to link people horizontally in a collaborative style, as well as vertically, can empower employees to deal with business issues effectively and can speed up their decisions and activities.

You must make it easy for your employees to make decisions that affect their work life and to take actions as quickly as possible. You also must empower your employees to work effectively in serving your customers. One way to do this is to make it easy for them to access information that will be of interest to your customers. Particular attention should be paid to linking information across departmental boundaries in a way that will help you better serve your customers. The Internet provides the most powerful way of getting information into your employees' hands.

It also will be critical to empower your customers. You'll want to make it easy for them to do business with your company. It sounds simple, but it's one of the things that companies most often overlook. You must make it easy for your customers to get information about your products and your company. You must make it easy for your customers to get answers to their questions wherever possible in a self-help fashion and make it easy for them to buy your products or services. Again, the Internet provides the speed and precision your company will need to ensure customer empowerment.

This means that you have to find engineering and design resources that can interact with your customer base in some meaningful fashion. Probably the most underused source of information comes from data gathered by tech support lines. I urge you to tap into this information and put it to work for your company.

I recall my days at Novell, when once or twice a year, our CEO, Ray Noorda, would actually man the support lines for a week. Ray was about 60 years old when Novell got started, and he retired when he was about 70. However, just about every six months, Ray would go out and sit among the employees in the tech support organization and answer phones along with the rest of the tech support team.

As you can imagine, people were pretty shocked when he'd answer the phone, "Hi, this is Ray Noorda. How can I help you?" Ray couldn't always solve the most difficult technical issues by himself, but this biannual process gave him a real sense of what was going on in Novell's business and how the customers felt about Novell's products.

Similarly, when I was working at Indiana University, I used to go out and man our tech support lines for two or three days a year. Frankly, some of the very best ideas I ever got about how to move our organization forward came from those days of listening to the issues to which our people found it difficult to respond. I hope that I didn't confuse too many students and colleagues with my questions and comments.

I think too often we use the Internet to isolate ourselves from our customers. We do this by putting product information, self-help aids, and order forms on the Internet. However, when the Internet is used to its best advantage, it really can connect us to our customers.

This means systematically "remembering" information about your customers and your relationship with them (of course, with their permission). It also means recalling that information every time you have contact with them in any way. You'll want to use the Internet to empower your employees and your customers, but don't forget about empowering your suppliers while you're at it.

You must make it easy for your suppliers to do business with you. Focus intently on empowering your suppliers and your employees who are working with your supply chain. I see far too many companies that are burdened by a misguided mission to preserve their legacy processes, not realizing that they are actually impeding their profit potential.

In today's business environment, I urge you to have a more open set of conversations with your suppliers and allow them to really deliver their full set of capabilities to your company. All too often we tie our suppliers' hands and then wonder why we're not as competitive as other companies working in our industry.

It's important to maintain good business objectivity, and you still can achieve this while letting your suppliers advise you, counsel you, and help you. This will allow your company to get the full value out of the partnerships you have.

In the Internet world, many companies, particularly technology providers, have much more to offer than they did in the past. If every vendor is treated through the eyes of the purely competitive bidding process, the benefits and advantages they have been working hard to create for you may never come to light.

To review, I suggest you follow this step-by-step examination of the way in which you focus on people:

- Examine the extent to which you have empowered your employees to make decisions as close to the customer as possible.
- Consider your organizational design and the technology you have in place to support that design.
- Make sure your employees have access to the knowledge or information they need for making good and timely decisions and that they are linked to colleagues who can help when issues extend beyond their individual responsibility. Ensure that those linkages are horizontal as well as vertical.
- Make sure your employees have the tools to implement their decisions quickly and effectively.
- Automate paper-driven processes wherever possible, but don't be afraid to work with paper at the boundaries of the organization to communicate with customers.
- Make sure your employees have access to the Internet because it will speed their ability to serve customers.
- Examine the extent to which you have empowered your customers.
- Use the Internet to enable your customers to access information about your company and your products quickly.
- Make sure you have used the Internet to its full potential so that your customers can have their questions answered in a self-help manner.
- Ask your executives to man your tech support phones periodically.

- Examine the extent to which you have made it easy for your suppliers to do business with you.
- Make sure your suppliers are delivering on their full set of capabilities, if necessary.

9.3 Driving All of Your Systems Toward Open Internet Systems

The key to making changes dynamically and quickly within your organization is to drive all of your systems toward open Internet systems.

A 2002 Business Information Processing Services (BIPS) study pointed out that, today, virtually all IT managers say they can no longer run their businesses without the Web because the Internet has become so integral to their businesses. The majority of these IT managers are still continuing to invest in Web-driven projects. This is a top-level affirmation that the Web-driven economic revolution is continuing, that its benefits are fundamental to business success, and that the Web is now touching businesses on a fairly widespread basis.

As you think about migrating toward Internet systems, remember that you can achieve this goal in a number of ways. One approach is simply to bolt on a frontend with a Web interface to the old terminal-driven interface you have been using. I've seen lots and lots of applications that look like that's exactly what's been done. The job was performed in a quick and dirty fashion, and it looks like it. The problem with this approach is that it doesn't help you achieve the productivity gains we've talked about earlier in this book.

Instead, I recommend that you consider more powerful connector architectures that will help you link your data with your processes. In the ideal world, you would be able to separate your business processes from your underlying data. That would allow you to develop the processes independent of the underlying data structures. Unfortunately, not a lot of applications are in a position to do that.

Then again, there are some powerful connecting architectures that will be a great help. HP has a free Applications Server (formerly Bluestone Total-e-server) you may want to consider. BEA Software is another company you should consider for help in this space if you want a more expensive and complete solution. Also, take a look at WebSphere from IBM.

The next thing I would recommend is that you take a look at the way applications are designed. You'll only get the full benefit of these applications if they deal with all of your processes systematically.

The exciting thing about the Internet is that you can use it to drive significant breakthroughs very, very quickly. An Internet deployment will allow you to achieve your first breakthroughs in 30 to 45 days as long as you have a good Web application developer. You also should be able to link your processes together in a meaningful fashion and dramatically improve the way that people interact with your Web environment.

This rapid-fire deployment is quite different than the way we used to do application deployment. Until recently, we spend months, or sometimes years, doing highly disciplined development, which included listening to customer feedback and making changes based on their comments.

The Internet has provided a totally different development environment that many people have yet to internalize. The new Internet model allows us to first get out a new application—fast—and then innovate continuously after it's out there. You can modify the application after you find out how people are using it and where they're getting hung up. Then, you can make changes on a daily basis, if you want. One of the greatest strengths of the Internet is that you can innovate with the customer on the fly, at any given moment. And your customer can be internal, external. or in your supply chain.

You'll need to make a commitment to rapid innovation because you'll be making lots of changes on the fly as you systematically harvest feedback and adjust your Web architecture accordingly. The good news is that you can rewrite your Web applications very quickly, so it won't be a terrible burden on your organization.

The Web tools available to your company will likely improve every six to nine months. If you're not updating your tools every year or two, you're just laying the foundation for disaster, so stay focused and stay current with your Web tools.

As far as deployment goes, keep in mind that you will be changing the way you're interacting with people. You'll also be changing the way you interact with legacy systems and the new systems you build.

These changes probably will change the performance characteristics of the applications you are using and your underlying communications architecture. They also will change the operating characteristics of the applications in some fairly fundamental ways. Therefore, I urge you to scrutinize your deployment every six to nine months as you fully examine your application design and architecture.

If you're systematic and disciplined in this cleanup process, you will continue to harvest the benefits of the rapid development capabilities of the Internet. The power of the Internet, of course, is that it offers you the ability to develop strategically relevant and important things very quickly.

In summary, to drive all of your systems toward open Internet systems, follow these steps:

- Consider using connector architectures that will help you link your data with your processes.
- Examine BEA Software, WebSphere, or HP's Application Server (HP-AS), or all three, for your systems migration work.
- Use applications that deal with all of your processes systematically.
- Prepare for rapid-fire deployment and results that can be quantified within 30 to 45 days.
- Innovate continuously.
- Make changes on the fly, as appropriate or necessary.
- Continuously harvest feedback and adjust your applications accordingly.
- Update your tools at least every year or two.
- Scrutinize your deployment every six to nine months.
- Commit to an ongoing, systematic, and disciplined approach to your cleanup and rewriting processes.

9.4 Focusing on Underlying Business Value Propositions

It's incredibly important to keep your focus on the underlying business value you are trying to deliver. In order to do this, you'll have to fully understand, and be able to articulate, your customer-value proposition.

Thanks to Internet technologies, you'll be able to continuously add to and innovate your customer-value proposition. For example, at HP we're touching close to 30 million people around the world each day, not just with our traditional HP products, but also in new and innovative ways. Our printer, scanner, and storage drivers are now available online to our customers—a fact that significantly enhances HP's customer-value proposition.

Even if your own company has as its primary offering a single product, you should think about how to use the Internet in some way to add more value for your customers. Of course, you can add to your underlying customer-value propositions in a million different ways, including the following:

- You can bring your products to market faster.
- You can reduce your cycle times.
- You can make your Web site more intuitive to navigate.

Some of the things you do will allow you to achieve intermediate targets that are nevertheless strategically important. However, they may not necessarily be directly and immediately driven into the customer-value proposition.

If you work in a services business or you sell intangibles like securities, it becomes all the more important that you stay focused on adding to your underlying customer-value propositions. Unfortunately, a good percentage of the time, you'll find that what you think is going to be extremely valuable to the customer isn't. Similarly, you will often find that things that you don't think will be particularly important end up being very hot in the eyes of your customer. The trick, of course, will be to deliver on things that your customers actually do value.

Here's a terrific example.

In 1968, Dr. Spence Silver, who was a research scientist at 3M, invented a slightly sticky and somewhat unusual adhesive. The adhesive formed itself into spheres as thin as paper fiber, but these spheres were almost indestructible. They wouldn't melt or dissolve and they were only slightly sticky. In short, 3M thought Dr. Silver's invention was pretty much useless, so, for six years, it sat on a shelf in the labs of 3M.

However, remember what I always like to say: Necessity is the mother of invention. In 1974, Art Fry, who was a 3M product development researcher, started thinking about Dr. Silver's sticky concoction when he was in church one day. Mr. Fry kept losing the bookmarks he had inserted into his choir book, and this was extremely frustrating to him. After church one day, Mr. Fry went back to the lab at 3M and splattered a bit of Dr. Silver's "unglue" onto a small piece of paper. To his utter delight, he had a made a bookmark for his book of hymns that could be positioned on any page and then easily removed and placed on yet another page. It was a masterstroke, so he thought.

Three years later, the upper management team at 3M remained unconvinced that Mr. Fry's idea would be of interest to customers. However, someone at 3M decided to do a little market testing by giving the 3M secretaries blocks of these new sticky notes without any instructions regarding their use. Naturally, the secretaries came up with thousands of uses for them, and a true product star was born. By 1990, 3M's Post-It Notes were one of the five top-selling office-supply products in the United States.

There is just no substitute for understanding your customers and understanding what they truly value. Therefore, if, for example, you decide to focus on improving your cycle times, I recommend making sure that your customers value that kind of rapid turnover in the market. For instance, HP has been able to chew up Sony's tailpipe when it comes to digital cameras. Sony recently had about 10 different digital camera models on the market. HP had two, and HP was outselling Sony. Sometimes less is more in the eyes of customers. Whereas Sony had banked its digital camera strategy on customers wanting endless choices in its product line, HP took a much more simplified approach to its digital camera strategy.

It turns out that your company can get itself into quite a dilemma if you overcomplicate your product portfolio. Ask yourself if you are creating churn in the cycle just for the sake of creating churn. Do you truly understood the ramifications of your churn rate and your cycle times in terms of meeting actual customer demands?

Another thing I've discovered is that the majority of one's cycle time is not actually spent generating the product, but rather it's spent thinking about what the team wants to do. These strategic decision-making cycles can be very difficult, indeed.

Quite often, people will focus on the engineering or technical side of product generation and work hard to reduce cycle times in those places. However, typically, that is not where the bottleneck occurs. Generally, greater reductions in cycle times can be gained by making decisions better and being able to recover from bad decisions faster.

Part of the whole process of focusing on underlying business-value propositions is to examine your supply chain issues carefully. I recommend that you do this at least on an annual basis, if not more often.

As you know, in the old days, we used to negotiate contracts with our supply chain that would last for two or three years. Nowadays, however, suppliers are hungrier than ever before, and they're reducing their own cycle times. They're also increasing their capabilities.

We're seeing more and more larger companies in the supply-chain business that are offering the kinds of economies of scale and enhanced design services that companies might not have been able to achieve previously.

Also, while you're busy focusing on your supply chain, make sure you also take a hard look at your transportation networks. As you may know, at HP, we've pretty much completely outsourced our imaging and printing repair supply inventory to UPS, which has saved us a fortune. It has also dramatically reduced the turnaround time for getting our products repaired in the field.

In summary, follow these steps as you endeavor to focus on your underlying business-value propositions:

- Continuously add to and innovate your customer-value proposition.
- Consider ways of using the Internet and Internet technologies to add more value for your customers.
- When appropriate and feasible, find ways to bring your products to market faster.
- When appropriate, reduce your cycle times.
- Establish intermediate and long-range targets.
- Make sure you're delivering things your customers actually want.
- Remember the Post-It Note case study and ask if there are any undiscovered hot products in your own research labs.
- Examine your supply chain at least every year.
- Negotiate shorter-term contracts with your supply chain.
- Take advantage of economies of scale whenever possible.
- Take full advantage of your transportation networks.

9.5 Rapidly Prototyping These New Value Propositions

As you consider your strategy for rapidly prototyping your new value propositions, keep in mind that the key to success is not to try to solve too many problems at one time. Don't make your projects too heavyweight. Carefully choose a project, rapidly prototype it, and launch it. If it works, scale up very quickly. If it doesn't work, you'll have the ability to trim it off quickly.

If you don't take this approach, it's very likely that you'll end up with an applications infrastructure that is almost impossible to maintain. As you may know, you can quickly end up maintaining lots of things that are not adding any strategic value to your business, yet are adding to the complexity of your applications infrastructure in other ways.

Therefore, focus on smaller, relatively lightweight exercises. This will limit your portfolio of risk-taking projects and the breadth at which you undertake application development. It also will increase your chances of long-term overall success.

A lot of companies run into trouble when they try to create big bureaucratic structures to decide which processes to work on next. All they seem to do is make it more and more difficult to get successive breakthroughs or improvements. By containing how big your experiments are, you can really prime your company for breakthroughs because you'll still have the resources to screen your experiments systematically and shut down those that aren't yielding the results you need.

I urge you to shut down the failed projects quickly. Don't let them drift on for a year or two, siphoning off additional company resources. If you're doing application development at the right pace, you'll have something up and running in three to four months. At that time, evaluate your results and immediately shut down failures and exploit successes.

I see more and more companies working on failing efforts for two or three years, even though absolutely no value is being gleaned from these efforts. In these cases, the development process is too slow, too big, and too cumbersome. Therefore, it's imperative that you remain flexible and agile as you experiment and invest on a smaller scale. As you probe and learn, you will undoubtedly land on tremendous breakthrough opportunities, which then can be pursued with a vengeance.

Learning to scale and enhance successes quickly is another success skill. Too often, scaling issues are not well thought through, and they become stumbling blocks to real success. In many cases, it is worth a rapid reengineering effort to put the technology on a scalable foundation after the initial customer or user breakthroughs have been achieved.

Also, be cautious that you don't reinvent the wheel every time you attempt one of these launch-and-learn experiments. At HP, we now have a team of deployment specialists who ensure that we're not making the same mistakes again and again. Because of this, our success ratio has increased dramatically.

Yahoo! also does a marvelous job with deployment. It has a team of people who have extensive expertise in working as coaches and consultants. Its limber approach to application deployment has allowed it to get products to market very fast and to scale up very fast when it has breakthroughs. Yahoo! is also relentless about its applications portfolio. If breakthroughs aren't achieved in six months, it shoots them. This has given Yahoo! the ability to cycle through new businesses and new opportunities at a faster pace than most companies.

In summary, these are the steps to take as you rapidly prototype your new value propositions:

- Don't try to solve too many problems at one time.
- Choose smaller, lightweight projects and then rapidly prototype and launch them.
- If your project is a success, scale up very quickly.
- If your project is a bust, kill it right away.
- Systematically redesign successes for scalability.
- Form smaller, SWAT-like groups to undertake these projects rather than involving large, bureaucratic structures to tackle the projects.
- Remain flexible and agile as you experiment and invest in these projects.
- Consider employing a small team of deployment specialists.

9.6 Looking for Additional Linkages Between Systems, Processes, and People to Create Even Greater Value

As I mentioned at the beginning of this chapter, often the solution to one problem can create an entirely new one. The problem you may very well encounter is that, when you do piecemeal, incremental breakthrough work, you may have a tendency to miss broader systematic improvements that you could make. Therefore, it is very important to look across all of your business processes in a meaningful fashion to see how new application deployments have impacted your entire business.

I like to call this process *harvesting*. Keep in mind that you'll want to harvest the applications and the technology, as well as harvest the deployment infrastructure. For example, when I was at Indiana University, we discovered that we had literally thousands of servers running different applications. Many of these servers were tucked away under people's desks. Indiana University was ahead of the Internet curve from 1993 through 1995. We were using the Internet in many, many ways, and the folks at Indiana University kept bringing new projects up very quickly. Before we knew it, we had a mission-critical process for the university running on a server that was sitting underneath somebody's desk. If this person inadvertently kicked the plug out, we were in deep trouble.

We had to come up with a solution, which we did when we physically pulled all of the servers back into a machine room. When we did that, we realized that we could consolidate a lot of these servers and thus improve our reliability. Then, we found that we could actually link some of our processes and even develop more powerful processes by actually rerouting a number of things that had previously been done separately and independently. This led us into the harvesting stage, where we were constantly reworking our processes and looking everywhere for ways to improve our processes and applications.

The point that I want to make here is that you must look beyond that proverbial server sitting under your desk for solutions that could well lie beyond your desk, your department, or even your entire company. This is a process that should be relentlessly pursued. Greater value can be reaped from almost any process, but you're going to have to systematically look for opportunities.

Don't be afraid to follow through with organizational and cultural changes. Often organizations will resolve customer issues primarily through referrals up the management chain. If the company's business processes have been redesigned, there will be more horizontal linkages that will allow individual employees to solve customer problems directly.

In summary, follow these steps as you look for additional linkages between systems, processes, and people to create even greater value:

• Keep your eyes open for ways in which incremental breakthroughs have impacted other processes within your organization.
• After each breakthrough, go back and carefully examine how broader, systematic changes can be achieved.
• Harvest your new applications and technologies to their fullest extent.
• Look for ways to reroute individual and separate processes so that they can be linked in a more meaningful and profitable fashion.
• Emphasize horizontal processes and cultural changes to empower employees.

9.7 Looking Beyond Your Organization's Boundaries for Other Partners and Solutions

One of the great, untapped resources in business today is the telecommunications industry. I am certain that telecommunications providers can offer a lot more value than most companies realize. If you are trying to build a business process that spans your organization and your suppliers, or reaches out to your customers in some fashion, leveraging an ensured telecommunications infrastructure can mean the difference between success and failure. Such a proven infrastructure can help you deal with security problems and communications problems in a way that will be entirely indispensable.

Many companies are still operating under the old model of objective, competitive bidding when it comes to securing outside resources to provide solutions. However, this approach can end up costing your company a good deal more. I recommend instead that you focus on working with dedicated, long-term partners who consistently look for ways to improve. More often than not, you'll find that these long-term partners can beat the old competitive bidding processes, hands down. However, if you feel you are not getting the kind of value you need from your long-term partners, by all means, rebid the work to others.

However, there is a risk that you could lose business objectivity by working with the same people over a long period of time. Therefore, combine these long-term, deep partnerships with a regular process of external benchmarking as has been done so successfully by the travel industry during the past several years.

Here's how the travel industry accomplished such a feat. It has offered bulk discounts to its large customers, while servicing those customers in a more integrated fashion. The industry has integrated both its frontend and backend systems, making it much easier for it to serve its corporate accounts. Sounds simple now, but it took some risk taking, a lot of thought, and a considerable amount of work. If you have the right telecommunications infrastructure in place, along with the right application deployment infrastructure, you'll be well on your way to the fast track to profit.

If changes with your partners are needed, I urge you to be honest and open. This is all part of a good partnership. Have a frank discussion about your concerns and see if there is a way to come up with a mutually acceptable solution.

There's a song from the musical *Mame* in which Mame's best friend sings, "Who else but a bosom buddy could tell you the god-awful truth?" Those lyrics have a lot of validity, and a lot that you can apply to your relationship with your partners.

Therefore, in conclusion, I recommend that you follow these steps as you look beyond your organization's boundaries for other partners and solutions:

- Look to your telecommunications providers for powerful solutions to your communications challenges.
- Look beyond the old model of objective, competitive bidding because better solutions might well be found among your long-term, trusted partners.
- Maintain a regular process of external benchmarking and discuss the results with your trusted partners.
- Be open and honest with your partners.

9.8 The Fast Track to Profit

Industry after industry has proven that it is possible to take the fast track to profit by systematically exploiting the world's best Internet technologies. The airline industry, for example, is certainly having its share of problems right now. However, if you look at the overall profitability history of the industry, many individual airlines have turned in strong profits until about a year ago. A lot of that success can be attributed to the way the airline industry drove systematic technology improvements throughout all of its processes. These efforts allowed the industry to control its costs and its yields.

Of course, September 11, coupled with the economic recession, has put a lot of pressure on the airline industry, and it now finds itself having profit troubles. However, most believe that these are temporary, and that the airline industry has built itself on a strong enough foundation, technologically speaking and otherwise, to survive these current tough times and to emerge profitable once again.

The auto industry, despite some of its own challenges, is much healthier today, due in great part to the way it has embraced the Internet revolution in its manufacturing and supply operations. The entire structure of the industry has dramatically changed, and this change would not have been possible without advances in networking.

However, keep in mind that there is no silver bullet that you can ride to the fast track to profit. It is my hope that, after reading this book, you will realize that business success happens when you work hard, stay focused, and concentrate on initiatives that are strategically relevant. In addition, you must have the discipline to prune out those things that just aren't working. You also have to have the discipline to go back and rework things on a systematic and periodic basis. If you're looking for a quick solution that you can ride for five years, you're going to be in trouble.

Success requires work and discipline. If you are looking for something for which you can deliver value in three to six months and then continuously innovate in that area, you're going to have a greater chance of finding yourself on the fast track to profit. You'll also have a much better chance of maintaining a sustainable competitive advantage and delivering sustainable value to your customers.

Finally, success requires that you be among the early adopters of new technologies. You don't have to be first, but, if you wait until you are in the middle of the pack, you will have passed up the opportunity to use the technology for strategic advantage. You also will not have the cost advantages your best-in-class competitor(s) are achieving.

Quite frankly, I believe that, if you follow the steps I've outlined in this book, your company can become much more profitable, and it will be a much more exciting and fun place to work.

And, speaking of fun, my economist friend loved to talk about the moments of fun that one could have on the tomato-canning assembly line. He said that several wonderful ladies worked on one part of that line, and it was their job to look for foreign objects among the tomatoes. They were experts at pulling out rocks and leaves and other debris that found their way onto the tomato-canning assembly line. You wouldn't believe, my friend said, how much fun one could have by occasionally tossing a rubber snake on the line.

After all, you know what they say about all work and no play...

Technology Primer for Executives

Let's face it. Most of today's executives are of such a vintage that there wasn't much of a structured Internet technology curriculum when they went through their Master of Business Administration (MBA) programs or their undergraduate business programs. Therefore, the odds are fairly high that they have a limited understanding of Internet technology and lingo. Moreover, until about 10 years ago, most academic business programs didn't require that students have more than a basic knowledge of telecommunications technology.

Even today, I've found that most mainstream business curricula are pretty spotty in their coverage of Internet and telecommunications technology. The problem is that many professors don't understand the technology that well, and most have no practical understanding of what it's like to actually deploy this technology in a meaningful way.

Of course, today's executives are not helped by the fact that some folks who work in the IT profession pride themselves on being the High Priests of Great Mysteries of the Universe, and they're not willing to share their knowledge. Therefore, if you're going to be a good general manager, you've got to have some sense of what your IT people are talking about.

I understand how embarrassing it can be to admit in front of IT people that you are running a high-tech company, but have no clue what your IT people are talking about. However, here's the good news. I believe you'll feel far more comfortable with the subject after you spend an hour or so reading through this Appendix. I can almost promise you that, before you can say, "By, George, I believe I've got it," you'll be able to throw out a few terms like "gigabit Ethernet technology" and "xHTTP" that will cause people's pupils to dilate more than a little bit.

One thing I've learned in my career is that, if you have a good understanding of basic technologies, you'll find it's pretty easy to track where technology is headed. However, if you try to follow technology through product announcements alone, you might find yourself baffled because product announcements are typically enveloped in marketing spin.

Now that you've read this guide on taking the fast track to profit, we're going to continue your postgraduate education in Internet and telecommunications technology. First, I'd like to suggest that you attend some seminars that are particularly designed for managers without a strong technology background. These seminars have a business and technology focus, which I believe you'll find to be very helpful. Following that, we're going to jump into the world of basic computer technology, so you'll feel more comfortable participating in discussion about Internet technology.

1. THE BENEFITS OF POSTGRADUATE TECHNOLOGY SEMINARS

If you are among those without a strong technology background, you might benefit from hearing from other executives in the industry who have great stories to tell about their own technology deployments. There is one particular rabble-rouser in the industry by the name of George Gilder. George runs a series of outstanding seminars called Telecosm. His Telecosm seminars are typically held each year at Squaw Valley, and attendees include executives from a variety of industries. Gilder's sweeping pronouncements should be taken with a grain or two of salt, however.

The Telecosm seminars have both a business and technology focus. The seminars are small and are attended by 200 to 300 executives each year. I've attended several of these, and I highly recommend them for any executive who is trying to get up to speed in the areas of networking and telecommunications. Trust me. Attend one of these seminars, and your mind will get expanded pretty vigorously. Through the years, I've dragged several other

IBM executives along with me, and they've each benefited greatly from the experience.

I've also found that the European Commission can be a great source of information. Because they have to work across so many countries in Europe, they tend to take the time to articulate technology policy issues better than most U.S. folks have. The European Commission has written a series of thought papers that provide very valuable insight.

I believe that the small price you pay early on to understand the various families of technologies can pay huge dividends throughout your career. As long as you understand the major families and architectures, you don't really need to spend your time chasing the products.

The Gartner Group also conducts a series of very valuable seminars and publishes many in-depth reports. Because the Gartner Group does not invest in companies they write about, they have an impartial, technology-sound perspective. Gartner analysts have many years of practical experience in addition to a broad industry perspective.

This knowledge will help you think more creatively about the kind of relationship you have with your customers and the way in which you're producing products and delivering services to your customers. If you reexamine those areas in light of new technology possibilities, you'll be incredibly empowered. You'll have a totally different perspective than you've had before. Your team will also get more productively engaged in moving forward and delivering more value to your shareholders and your customers.

2. THE VOCABULARY OF BASIC COMPUTER TECHNOLOGY

Now let's jump into the world of Internet technology by starting off with a description of **HTML**.

HTML stands for Hypertext Markup Language. Before the widespread use of HTML, people produced content with word processors, and it was difficult to convert content between the various types of processors. As the Web came into being, it became obvious that a more general set of formatting tools was required, and the industry adopted HTML.

If you look at a standard Web page through the "view source" function of your browser, you can see what hypertext looks like. On most Web pages, it is a confusing set of cryptic-looking codes enclosed in brackets like this: <

>. These codes contain basic information about what to display and where to display it. Think of HTML as the hidden codes that tell the computer how words and objects should be displayed on the computer screen.

If you were an old WordPerfect user, you may remember that it had a function called Reveal Codes. If you went into the Reveal Codes mode, you could see hidden codes, such as: "bold" and "end bold," "center this," or "put a table here." Today, most word processing software can read and produce HTML documents, and there are hundreds of specialized tools for creating these codes that the browser then uses to render the output on the screen.

A **browser** is a computer tool that helps you access and display things on the Internet. It's the vehicle through which you view HTML and other Internet-based pages. Microsoft's Internet Explorer or Netscape Navigator are examples of browsers.

With HTML, you can display things graphically on the screen. The ability to include graphics was one of the big breakthroughs of the browser. With the old terminal emulators, you couldn't display graphics at all. Everything had to be explained in words.

Behind the scenes today, there is something called **http**, or hypertext transport protocol. When you type "http://" and then you type a Web address, you are transported to your desired Web site. The Web address is called the Universal Resource Locator (**URL**). For example, the Internet address of HP's Web site is http://www.hp.com. In most Web browsers, you don't have to type in the http portion of the address, but, if you look at the address line of the browser, you will see that the browser has inserted the http:// for you. HTML also allows you to link into other **Web pages** or **URLs**. The HTTP code is basically what allows you to make those kinds of linkages.

Now, HTML was fine when you were assuming that you were going to display things on a computer screen. Most computer screens are roughly the same size and have similar aspect ratios.

Today, many Web pages contain **Extensible Markup Language** (**XML**) codes. XML is a simple markup language used for representing documents. Many Web pages also contain embedded Java programming language code that can actually link the browser client to servers elsewhere in the environment.

XML is a language in which you can write HTTP documents that can format content to meet the requirements of a specific device, like a PDA. XML offers great data processing and display independence. XML is intended to allow more fine-grained marking of parts of the documents, by identifying with tags the various document contents.

When working with XML and HTML, you'll encounter **style sheets**. Style sheets contain the roadmaps for various device capabilities. You can use XML to send basic information about your display characteristics. The style sheet can translate your preferences to the particular device.

The other thing that XML enables is the ability to merge data, text, and graphics in a better fashion. If you look at traditional Web pages, you'll see that programmers may have done some limited things with the Java programming language in order to make those Web pages more active. There's a good chance that programmers have included little pull-down menus, for example, so that, when you start typing in a state name, the state names pop in with their two-letter state initials.

The **xHTML protocol** allows you to print directly from your devices. If you look at a PDA screen, you certainly wouldn't want a printout the size of a postage stamp. With XML or xHTTP and a style sheet, you'll be able to print your PDA image from a nice printer and get a great looking printout.

We've had a hard time in HTML and in the Web environment at making screens interact with individuals the way that we wish they could. The next waves of the technology revolution are likely to bring screens that are more intelligent and more interactive than they are today.

For the most part, when you interact with an HTML screen today, you're putting information into it, perhaps by filling in all the information requested of you. Then you send the entire screen. Much too often, you'll get a message back that says, "You blew it! You left fields blank, or you put in an invalid point." This really is an ugly way to interact with users. I hope that as we move forward on the XML front, Web designers will create ways for users to have more friendly interactions with their sites.

Next, I'd like to shed some light on the mechanics of **Internet technology**. The fundamental technology driving the Internet is what is called **packet switching**. Packet switching is the term used to characterize the manner is which data is broken up into variable length packets.

Data is chopped up into small pieces as it's sent across the Internet. Internet **switches** can handle lots of data from lots of people simultaneously. To accomplish this successfully, the packets must be created on the sending side and reassembled on the receiving side into streams of data. **Routers** queue the packets of data on the Internet. Each packet has an **addressing header** on it, which points the packet in the right direction on the Internet.

The routers maintain **routing tables** that are basically a list of the next destinations through which data needs to be sent. These tables don't necessarily have to resolve the packets all the way out to their final destinations, but they do resolve the packets as far as the next destination to which they should be sent.

There is an actual protocol for this process, and it's called **Open Shortest Path First**. On each step of the way, the routers are dynamic. They're intelligent. They're self-healing. They update the routing tables dynamically, and paths can be created dynamically between various routers. There is also Border Gateway Protocol and IS-IS for these purposes. What this means is that, if a particular link is down, the routers can find other ways of getting data where it needs to go. It's very hard to crash or kill the Internet.

If you compare the structure of the Internet to the structure of the telephone network, you'll discover that 1) the telephone network is made up of a number of very large, very expensive switches that are all interconnected, and 2) the Internet is made up of literally millions of tiny routers, the largest of which is much smaller than the average cell phone switch. There is not nearly as much intelligence in an Internet router as there is in these big telephone switches, and the big telephone switches and routers are loaded with software.

A router is highly specialized. Router algorithms are fairly effective and efficient. Because the packets are broken into small pieces, you end up with queues being formed inside the routers as they route data on its way.

One of the things about routers that cause problems with telecommunications traffic is a situation we call **latency** or **delay**. Latency or delay occurs when the queue lengths become elongated and the packets aren't passing through with their normal lightning speed or if the speed of any underlying link is too slow. One way to deal with latency problems is overprovisioning, where you lease enough high-speed capacity to meet your greatest peak needs.

The Internet hardware industry continues to develop new technologies to improve the overall effectiveness of bandwidth use. To cope with latency issues, new integrated **switch-routing technologies** have been invented. Switching allows larger bandwidth pipelines between major portions of the Internet that are getting higher spread usage. When demand on particular routers increases, switching technologies can ease the burden. At its core, all networking involves **queue theory**: how you deal with managing long lines of packets waiting to be routed.

Most Internet service providers have a unique **backbone**. They have a backbone of either leased or owned lines that they use to route their core data across. Not all ISPs have a backbone—many are just access providers. With average Internet use, you might be crossing the backbones of several providers. There are a number of major **cross-connection points,** as shown in Figure A-1. These cross-connection points were basically set up back in 1995. Originally, the federal government provided some of the funding for these cross-connection points. There are now scores of such Internet Exchange Points.

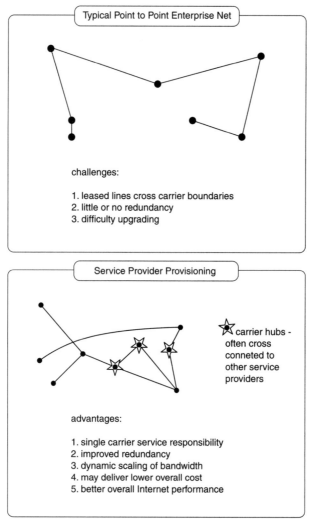

wide area network architectures

Figure A-1   WAN architectures.

The granddaddy backbone, the ARPANET, was used from 1975 to 1990 as the primary backbone of the Internet in the United States. NSFNET was the next big backbone, and after 1994, there were a number of commercial backbones. You'll recall that I discussed ANS in Chapter 6. The ANS Internet backbone was run by MERIT at the University of Michigan, and later by the ANS organization on MCI circuitry, which ran at 45 megabits per second. Eventually that ANS backbone was sold to AOL.

Meanwhile, other vendors like MCI, Sprint, and AT&T, and a number of other private companies, came in and set up their own Internet backbones. The federal government wanted to encourage competition in the Internet backbone space, so it provided a limited amount of funding for a short period of time to be used to create cross-connection points.

Various companies managed the cross-connection points. There was one in Chicago, one in New York, one in Washington, D.C., and a couple out on the west coast. Today, the vendors run those cross-connection points themselves and have developed a number of private cross-connection points.

The challenge with the cross-connection points is that it would be preferable to have vendors' equipment collocated, or set side by side. You would typically like to route the data or the packets using high-speed local area networking technology as opposed to wide area networking technology.

Quite often you'll have a number of vendors' routers in the same facility. These routers are connected with **gigabit Ethernet technology**. This is the same kind of technology you would use in a corporate enterprise environment to handle your cross-connection needs.

From an executive's point of view, it's probably more important to understand the economics that these technologies enable, rather than to understand how the underlying technology actually works. From an economics point of view, I urge you to give your primary telecommunications provider a chance to bid its own telecommunications infrastructure whenever possible, as opposed to having to cross the boundaries between the various service providers. This will allow both your company and your primary telecommunications vendor to control your costs more effectively. Your primary telecommunications provider also will be able to leverage and scale its own underlying bandwidth better than if you require your vendor to span boundaries.

Inevitably, however, you'll need to cross some boundaries. Therefore, when you look at procuring telecommunications services, it's important to give your vendor the chance to deploy things into its **Points of Presence (POPs)** as much as possible, in order to leverage its POP infrastructure and its backbone infrastructure. POPs are where the vendors or the **Internet Service Providers (ISPs)** have their major backbone routers.

Most vendors have dedicated fiber optic bandwidth between their POPs. Therefore, if you can run across their backbone, the vendor can have a fixed annual cost for operating the background. Thus, the vendor can give you a better deal on your telecommunications costs.

Another part of the POP puzzle involves the issue of getting data from corporate or business locations into the POPs. To do that, you typically **lease lines**, typically from the prime service provider with whom you contract. At the end of the day, you want that vendor to be responsible for your overall service quality. Also, the prime vendor usually has wholesale or volume purchasing power you may not have.

When you do that, you'll be trading off leasing lines locally versus using the POP connectivity infrastructure. This happens most often when you lease lines in **Local Area Tariffs (LATAs)**. Even though you might be working with a regional Bell operating company, it's important to know that they have multiple LATAs within the regional Bells. This is basically where you pay for long distance intrastate calls versus local calls.

If you start crossing LATA boundaries, the lease line charges typically go up quite a bit. A good telecommunications engineer has to be able to balance running some lines across those inter-LATA boundaries versus the POP locations. In addition, you may actually sublease Internet capacity from a carrier who may have POPs in that location and who uses cross-connection points.

The fact of the matter is that procuring basic Internet services is a more complicated thing than most people realize. Often, I find that computer companies, or people procuring computer services, tie the hands of the service providers in such a way that the service providers are boxed into a corner where they simply can't offer the customer a very good rate.

Let's move on now, to talk about the way in which services are actually procured.

If your company has high demands, one of the things you can do is procure a **leased line**. In this case, you typically procure at least a **T1 circuit** that handles 1.44 megabits per second, a **T3 circuit** that handles 45 megabits per second, an **OC3 circuit** that handles 155 megabits per second, or an **OC12** circuit that handles 622 megabits per second. If you have a smaller organization with lower demands, a simple Digital Subscriber Line (**DSL**) may do the trick.

You can procure just about any capacity. The problem you'll have to wrestle with is that Internet traffic tends to be very bursty. In other words, you may have an average demand that can be handled by a T1 circuit, but, occasionally, you'll experience demand that will require a burst of up to 10 megabits per second. However, these bursts only occur during certain hours of the day or when you have such things as a new product introduction. To meet these uneven demands, a growing trend in telecommunications is to procure what is called a **base rate with a burst rate**.

Among the technologies that have allowed that to occur is something we call **frame relay**. Frame relay is just a way of overlaying data services on a big network. This allows you, for example, to have a base rate of T1 with a burst rate of 3T1s. This is less expensive than procuring a T3. Instead, you could use three T1s simultaneously and save money in doing so. Keep in mind that one T3 = 28 T1s, not 3 T1s.

Europe uses similar types of circuits, but they have different names than the U.S. circuits. For example, in Europe, you have **E1 circuits** as opposed to T1 circuits. E1 circuits handle about 2 megabits per second as opposed to 1.544 for the T1s in the U.S. Europe's E1 circuits handle 30 voice lines as opposed to the 24 lines that T1s handle.

In both geographies, the frame relay and the burst rate have enabled a **committed data rate** that allows a more flexible kind of pricing structure. The economics of a committed data rate will often allow you to move up to a T3 for about the same price as if you're buying three or four T1s. You'll just have to look at the economics involved, and decide whether pure leased-line circuits, a committed data rate, a burst rate combination, or a higher capacity leased line makes the most sense for your company.

Next, it will be time to take a hard look at your **Internet architecture**. This is an area where many corporations make serious mistakes.

Many corporations, for example, will carry a fair amount of traffic in parts of the network where it probably doesn't make sense. A good vendor or a good networking shop will have **protocol analyzers** that they put online to analyze the nature of the applications that are generating traffic. This information needs to be monitored on an ongoing basis to get some sense of where your traffic is coming from, and to do appropriate balancing in response.

Quite often, people will blindly buy more bandwidth, even when it's not needed. Before they know it, they end up with the wrong application infrastructure in place, and they're running up costs and making their network traffic problems worse. The irony is that many of these problems are caused when companies add unneeded bandwidth to their Internet architecture.

Let's also discuss some of the underlying technology found in the **typical telecommunications infrastructure**. Most enterprises and some homes tap into what are called **Local Area Networks**, or **LANs**. LANs are very inexpensive to deploy, and they carry data at very high speeds.

Ethernet technology is what is used in most LANs. Ethernet speeds can go all the way up to 10 gigabits per second. The current popular standard is one gigabit per second, and you'll find this in widespread use in corporate data centers, for example.

The typical desktop computer today has about 100-megabit-per-second capacity. Most desktops tap into what we called **switched Ethernet** technology. It used to be that Ethernet technology was called a **shared media**, where everybody on the cable had access to 10 megabits per second. That was the original Ethernet standard. Under this standard, everybody competed for the 10-megabit-per-second traffic. Most cable TV Internet offerings also use shared media technology.

Today, the Ethernet standard is 100 megabits per second, and virtually everybody has a dedicated 100-megabit-per-second link back into the switching port. Quite often, a gigabit-per-second Ethernet will be deployed on the back plane to connect all of these switches and then to connect them into a routing infrastructure. In some cases, you may deploy routers rather than switches in the closets to pass traffic between the various segments of the network.

From an applications point of view, the problem we experience is that a lot of our applications were deployed for the LAN environment. While I was working at Novell, I spent six years of my life telling everybody that LANS and network operating systems were the greatest things since sliced bread. Of course, back then, they were.

LANs and network operating systems were designed around a workgroup model. With these, you took a file server of some sort, and everybody in the workgroup shared files on that server and shared printing resources, as shown in Figure A-2. People within a workgroup located in the same geographic location could share files relatively easily. Back in those days, hard disk storage was at a premium, and people tended to store their application software out on the server so that they had more storage available locally for their individual files.

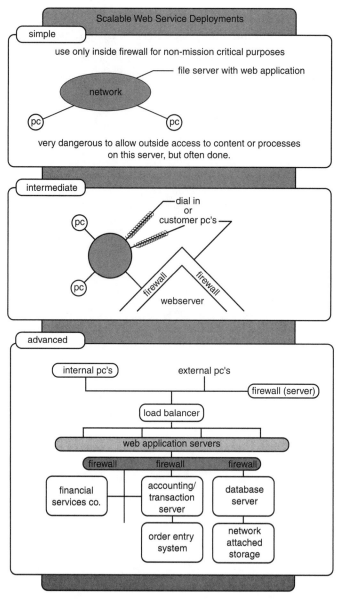

Figure A-2   Scalable Web service deployments.

The LAN environment in the workgroup model was really a powerful new paradigm that took the standalone PC and placed it into a workgroup productivity solution. It was a paradigm that worked extraordinarily well for 15 years.

The problem today is that corporations have extended workgroups that work across the enterprise in different geographies. The original workgroup model was designed to work within a geographically close space where bandwidth was free. The traditional client/server environment, for many companies, has not been able to scale the way it's needed. The multiple server environment was one "solution" that caused more problems than it fixed.

Today, of course, a classic workgroup infrastructure can span the globe, and many companies are still trying to use outdated protocols to move information around. Their file server protocols are very chatty, and they don't scale as well as the companies had hoped.

Another problem companies are experiencing is that the overhead associated with maintaining their file servers and user lists administratively can be a nightmare. That's why **global directories** were invented.

One other problem that companies are experiencing is that the nature of the applications that people are using has shifted considerably because of the Internet and because of the shift in competing hardware. That has allowed, for example, **extremely high-capacity storage** to be available on almost anything. We're now into the gigabytes of storage available on almost any device you can buy. Imagine. Today, HP is putting a full gigabyte of storage on its PDAs. For about $50, you can add 128 kilobytes on a PDA by adding a flash memory card.

With a gigabyte on the average PDA, we're going to have a very different game going forward. Even with a portable or a desktop PC today, you can barely even find a system that has less than 16 or 20 gigabytes of storage. Therefore, it doesn't make sense anymore to store all of your application information out on file servers. Today, we tend to use networking instead to connect into business processes that often involve linking bigger machines into **Web servers, applications servers,** or **email servers**, as shown in Figure A-3.

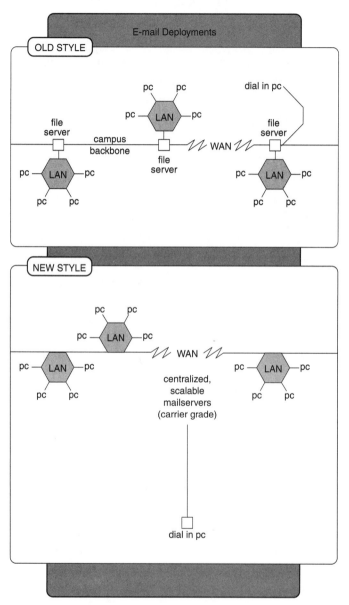

Figure A-3   Email deployments.

Email servers also work very differently than the old file servers did. With email servers, we have a store-and-forward kind of architecture. Web servers collect data and also do a whole lot of retrieval and uploading for you. We also have about 10 times as much traffic coming down the Internet to the client as there is traffic moving back up to the Internet. As you can imagine, there was a much more balanced load between the client and the server in the old client/server model days.

As expected, today's environment has radically changed the pattern of how **applications** are deployed. If you look at the average enterprise today, you'll typically find a workgroup **file-and-print infrastructure**. Most workgroup environments today, including HP's, are largely built around the file service model.

When people in a corporate environment today log on to their desktop computers, they typically use a dialogue login function that connects them to a number of file servers. There is typically a good deal of background chatter on these networks, which is why many of them run so poorly.

Many companies have tried to install a **Windows NT environment**, but it, too, has a very chatty client/server kind of architecture. I think it's an obsolete architecture, and, for the most part, companies don't need that kind of infrastructure anymore. HP has done wonders to simplify this administrative environment with its PC COE desktop management system. It does not, however, address the underlying applications infrastructure with its corresponding network traffic implications.

Unfortunately, the stuff I spent six years of my life telling everybody was the greatest thing since sliced bread is actually of limited or no value anymore. I suppose that's just the nature of technology! When it comes to technology, you ought to remember this. As communications capacity shifts and as processor and storage capacity shifts, the way we get things done will shift substantially.

In a nutshell, if you're standing still in the world of technology, you're actually falling behind.

Many companies have mainframe architectures in place with a legacy set of applications for which they have spent millions and millions of dollars. Typically, companies have built their accounting, financial, human resource, order-entry, and inventory management systems around this mainframe architecture. As you know, these core business processes are quite often done on some sort of big iron or a mainframe.

Some companies have taken the step to move to a client/server architecture that is running on top of UNIX. IBM, HP, and BEA have done a good job of providing connector architectures from that environment into the Java programming language environment.

At the very least, you could put a Web frontend onto your mainframe architecture and do something called **screen scraping**. Screen scraping allows you to take an application that used to run off of a terminal and put a Web interface on it. Instead of running on a proprietary terminal with proprietary networking, you could substitute a standard Web browser interface and still interact with the application, as though you were on a terminal. You also no longer need to be running IBM 3270 terminal emulation software.

That transition occurred in about 1996, when the first dedicated desktop terminals appeared. Then we moved to terminal emulation that enabled a 3270 terminal emulator to run across Internet protocols. Next we moved to screen scraping and to the browser.

The most current step has been to Java-enable your data so you can start putting the interaction with the host application together in a more dynamic, flexible architecture. This also allows you to link your data into other new and evolving applications and processes.

Companies that have taken this final step now have a multitier architecture that includes a mainframe with a UNIX server in front of it. That UNIX server can do the screen scraping and send out the HTML scripts that you need to interact on the terminals. This is a lot cheaper and a lot less complex than maintaining terminal emulation software out on every PC. Basically, a $3 billion software market for terminal emulation software disappeared overnight. One problem, of course, is that these are multisystems processes, and, when one of the systems crashes, the whole application can crash.

With the rapid development of the Internet has come the development of some new tools that allow companies to manage their core development databases more easily. Oracle and DB2 are dominant players in this space. Oracle owes a great deal of its success to the fact that it embraced the Internet early on and developed scalable tools that allowed its customers to work more effectively.

A big and powerful enterprise application may actually have its own high-end server. One of the most processor-intensive activities in which a company might engage is running its database server architecture on the backend. In those instances, you may actually have the application logic running on yet another server. This is quite often something like the Java programming language. The application would then be written in the Java programming language, and it would make the database calls that would be handled by the database servers. In some cases, you would use another architecture, such as Microsoft's Windows NT architecture, that would be doing the actual client interfaces and creating the HTML code that would go out to the browsers in some fashion. Funny thing is, by the time you've created your technology environment, you could very well end up with three or four servers sitting between you and your application data.

Oh, yes, you'll also have to be concerned about security problems. After you put security measures in place, you'll need firewall servers and data-extracting applications. You certainly won't want your clients interacting with the data you are maintaining for the integrity of your business, so you'll need to do data extracts to put sensitive data onto another server.

That server will be connected to a firewall, and then you'll have a firewall between the Internet and your application environment. By the time you're finished creating a secure environment, you can easily end up with three or four layers of firewalls around your processes.

Brace yourself, because the bottom line is that you could literally end up with dozens of servers running a single set of applications. Compare this to the old days, when terminals were connected back into a single computer. Maybe you had a frontend processor that helped you serve more terminals simultaneously. However, today, we've evolved into very complex IT infrastructure environments that most folks have not taken the time to completely think through. When this happens, you'll typically have an IT mess on your hands.

Because of this eventuality, I strongly suggest that you systematically, and every six months, evaluate your IT infrastructure. These environments can get away from you in a hurry because new functionality is developed so quickly. If you have the freedom of easy scalability, you can easily add 40 or 50 servers in no time flat.

When that happens, you can often collapse some of that functionality into a simpler function, using a more powerful and scaleable box of some sort. Your deployment costs can actually show a full Return on Investment (ROI) in a matter of months.

A number of hosting companies have been springing up during the Internet revolution. One of the original hosting companies was Exodus.

Qwest also has had global hosting centers, and so did Level3 and Global Crossing. Global Crossing actually sold its hosting center to Exodus to raise cash. Soon thereafter, Exodus went bankrupt. A lot of hosting operations have been betting on the hope that they were going to get effectiveness and efficiency breakthroughs by operating large numbers of servers.

What these hosting companies discovered is that it is incredibly difficult to deal with the complexity of application deployment in large-scale environments. As you may know, HP has been trying to simplify this task by employing a utility data center model that can automate a fair amount of the work involved in application deployment and management. IBM has a similar product called eLiza and is now shipping a server that is enabled. HP, on the other hand, is actually shipping its Utility Data Center. It's an architecture that supports both Solaris and HP/ux, as well as EMC's and HP's storage architectures.

As I've looked at many of the data center management tools over the years, I've found a fair number of firms that buy these tools, but don't deploy them. What a surprise. These data center management tools don't do much good if they just sit on the shelf. Therefore, if you're suffering from application reliability problems, servers crashing all the time, and slow recovery times, you should be thinking about employing more sophisticated management data architectures.

With the **telecommunications technology**, you are no doubt familiar with traditional wired technologies, such as copper, fiber, and wire link. **Wireless technologies** travel through the **radio frequency spectrum**. Satellite technologies fall into one of three categories: **Low-Earth Orbiting (LEO)**, **Middle-Earth Orbiting (MEO)** and **Geo-Synchronous** (GEO), as shown in Figure A-4.

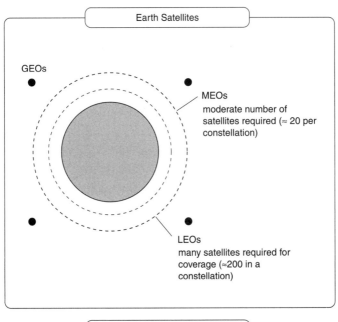

Earth Satellites

GEOs

MEOs
moderate number of
satellites required (≈ 20 per
constellation)

LEOs
many satellites required for
coverage (≈200 in a
constellation)

generations of wireless service

1	analog	N/A	N/A	Voice
2	digital	14.4 kbs	CDMA/GSM	Voice
2.5	digital		CDMA/GPRS	Voice/Data
3	digital	2 megabits/sec.	CDMA/UMTS	Voice/Data/Video

Figure A-4   Earth satellites and generations of wireless service.

The GEO satellites have been the ones that we've traditionally used for communications, such as DirectTV systems. They are placed above the orbit of the Earth, and in an orbit high enough so their rotation and orbit exactly match the rotation speed of the Earth. That means that they are more or less stationary in orbit.

The problem with GEO satellites is that there are only a few spots in the sky that you can use these types of satellites. That is because there are only a few places where you can get coverage across a particular continent. Therefore, there is a huge amount of competition to put satellites in those GEO orbits. In the United States, the FCC controls where the coverage can be, and, in Europe, there is a similar commission. There is also an international organization that tries to coordinate these satellites across other continents as well. Most of the work of these commissions involves issuing broadcast licenses and controlling the positioning of the satellites. Interestingly, there are some new technologies that have allowed us to increase the number of satellites in orbit around the GEO points.

One of the advantages of GEO coverage is that you have very broad coverage over a continent. The satellite is always in position, so you have a fairly good and reliable kind of service. The disadvantages of GEO coverage include the fact that the satellites are quite far from Earth, so you're likely to have huge latency or delay going up and down. With voice traffic, this produces a huge echo effect. On computers, it can cause the application to think the connection is lost, so it times out.

In the case of TV broadcasts, this latency issue is not a problem because the data is just being sent one way. You're actually streaming data off of the satellite. As long as the data stream isn't interrupted, you'll end up with a good TV signal.

If you're listening to a live broadcast from an Earth station or a local radio station, and simultaneously listening to a satellite broadcast, there will be a several-second delay in the signal. This is because the signal has to shoot all the way to the satellite and then all the way down to the Earth at 186,000 miles per second. That's the speed limit in space, you know! We haven't figured out a way around this delay because of how high in orbit the satellites sit.

Traditionally, a lot of these birds had a low power output, so they needed huge Earth station antennas. With DirectTV, we now have higher-powered satellites in orbit, so the antennas on our homes and businesses can be much smaller.

Our middle orbiting satellites and the lowest orbiting satellites were designed to deal with the problems of latency. However, the LEOs and the MEOs are hard to keep in orbit. You must continuously add power to them, unlike the GEO birds that you can just put up there and leave alone for a good long time.

The LEOs are the most problematic because they're closer to Earth, and, as such, their orbits decay more rapidly due to the gravitational pull the Earth exerts on the satellites. You must continuously relaunch the satellites, and it takes more of them to cover the surface of the Earth. They also require more complicated technology on the ground because you have to track them constantly because they won't stay in a single orbiting position.

One example of an MEO that we use a lot is the GPS system. There is a database in the global positioning satellite receiver that identifies where the satellites' stations are located in your geographical area. At any given time, you can usually link into three to five of the GPS stations. They have made getting lost virtually a thing of the past. Getting lost may no longer be a problem, but having too many people trying to access a single satellite frequency can be a problem.

Historically, there has been just one frequency that covers an entire continent. **Frequency clots** occur when you're trying to use a single frequency for two-way communication. **Spot beam** technology actually shoots narrow signals with cells, somewhat like we do with cell phones operating on different frequencies. Spot beam is an evolving technology that is likely to get very popular in the future.

There also have been several new **land-line technologies** developed recently. One of these is called **Dense Wave Division Multiplexing (DVDM)**, wherein we've been able to split live frequencies into various colors, with each of the colors carrying the capacity of the line when it is only white light.

Meanwhile, the price of **fiber optic repeaters** has fallen dramatically during the last four years, from about $30,000 each to less than $300 each. That has allowed the deployment of a lot more fiber a lot more cheaply than ever. That's why so many big national and intercontinental works got pulled so rapidly. Entry barriers disappeared when the cost of fiber-optic repeaters plummeted.

Terrestrial wireless also has provided huge technological improvements in cellular technology.

One of the challenges in the telecommunications industry is that the U.S. government has taken over so much of the radio frequency spectrum that it makes it very difficult for businesses to be agile with their approach to the deployment of services on a worldwide basis. There are far more European wireless cell phone users than there are in the U.S., and the cost of provisioning services in Europe is lower than it is in this country. This is because Europe has a standard set of technologies and frequencies, and their phones work well in the rest of the world, except in the United States where we're incompatible. For Americans, the lesson to be learned here is that compatibility breeds success. Incompatibility breeds chaos.

During the past decade or so, I've observed a pattern in the way technology evolves. This insight should provide some comfort to you because you'll be pleased to know that you don't have to chase every facet of technology all of the time.

In terms of **network infrastructure**, it takes about five years for major technology trends in Internet networking products to work themselves through the industry. Unfortunately, a lot of people got hung up thinking that this was a six-month cycle, but it really takes about five years for a pervasive change to take place in this space.

Therefore, if you look at wire speed routing, for example, this technology was first being talked about in 1995 or so. It wasn't until a few years later that wire speed routing hit the market. Still, there are many companies that are not using this powerful technology yet; instead they are relying upon lower speed routing technology.

The adoption curve for network infrastructure technology is about five years, but, when it comes to Internet technology, I highly recommend that you make sure that your company is included among the first third of adopters. You don't want to be lagging, and you definitely don't want to be among the final third of adopters. If you're lagging behind and in that final category, that means you're missing huge market opportunities to be more efficient, to be more cost-effective, and to have strategic advantages that your competitors may not have. If you delay, all you have is the expense of upgrading without the strategic advantages of your more aggressive competitors.

Therefore, help pave your way on the fast track to profit by exploiting Internet technologies early. If you're exploiting these technologies for economic efficiency or for competitive purposes, you simply cannot afford to be much beyond the first half of adopters.

I find it remarkable how many companies say that they don't want to be on the leading edge of technology. I can assure you that, when it comes to network hardware, in particular, you do want to be nearer the leading edge than the middle of the pack and as far from the tail end of the pack as you can be. Companies that are late adopters of Internet technologies are finding themselves in trouble at the end of the game.

Another technology curve you'll want to consider is in the **applications** space. Please note that there is a different technology curve for client and for server backend technologies. For back-end server technologies, there's about a five-year cycle. The Java programming language actually percolated around for many years before it was publicly announced by Sun. IBM had eight internal projects similar to the Java programming language, but, understanding the value of true interoperability, abandoned these and embraced Java. Oracle did the same thing. These two software giants and their customers benefited from this major step toward interoperability.

In the field of technology, it's quite often the case that several companies start working on developing a new product category at the same time. The reason for this is that, as the state of the art advances, scientists and engineers with common backgrounds will identify a common set of problems at about the same and will apply the emerging technologies to those problems.

If you're a seasoned technologist, you know that there tend to be similar approaches to solving problems. Therefore, you won't be surprised to discover the same kinds of technologies springing up in a number of places, more or less simultaneously. This can happen on a global basis. In Europe, Asia, and the United States, you may find many companies working on the same set of issues on a daily basis and not communicating with each other at all.

The strategic decision by IBM created the momentum the industry needed to have the Java programming language adopted on a wide-scale basis. It's important to recognize that, especially in the area of Internet technology, the power of collaboration can help get products to market faster.

How exactly, do you know that the time is right to migrate to a new technology?

One of the best things you can do is keep your head in your industry, especially from an IT point of view. You must keep an eye on what your competitors are doing. This will be crucial if you want to stay on the leading edge and be an industry innovator, or even a fast follower.

Remember, in the Internet space, you either have to be the breakthrough innovator or a very fast follower. The middle of the pack comes along very quickly, and the trailing edge is often gobbled up alive.

You need to constantly keep an eye on the technology in use by your competition. That's a hard thing to do because, quite often, you don't realize that they've had a major technology innovation until you're roadkill. Therefore, keep your market intelligence folks on high alert.

Another key area on which you should focus is using the Internet to research what your competitors are doing. More and more companies are disclosing on their Web sites what they're doing from a technology point of view. You'll often be able to read about their strategic efforts in their public 10K reports. It's surprising how much information about technology many companies put in their 10Ks these days. Never underestimate the value of ongoing, competitive intelligence to gauge the state of the art in your industry. A lot of this information is right in the public domain.

Another thing I would recommend is that you pick another couple of industries to study. Choose industries that are more technologically advanced than yours. Monitor their activities, their strategies, and their successes.

One of the problems in the insurance industry is that insurance companies have been so busy looking at one another that they haven't had time to take a look at what's been happening in the far more advanced financial services industry and the travel industry. As a result, insurance companies have been real laggards in the field of technology advancement. That is costing the insurance industry billions of dollars each year in terms of cost efficiency related to the kinds of interactions they have with their customers.

Keep in mind that, if you just spend your time in your own comfortable club, you're going to be missing major market opportunities. That approach will make you very vulnerable to a technology disruption when one of your competitors really does get the formula and achieves a major breakthrough.

Such a breakthrough can often leave the rest of the industry in shambles, almost overnight.

If you need some guidance in this area, you might want to contact some of the industry analysts' groups, such as The Gartner Group. They do a whole series of comprehensive reports of technology areas. They also offer very helpful seminars for executives. I know a lot of customers who have benefited greatly from the rigor and intelligence that The Gartner Group brings into this space.

However, you must be prepared. The folks who work for The Gartner Group don't pull any punches. They have a well-deserved reputation for rigor on a broad range of technology issues. You are bound to hear things that may make you uncomfortable.

I wouldn't bet your company on a Gartner Group report. They don't always get things right, but nobody working in technology ever gets everything right. Therefore, be sure to tap into an array of inputs to your strategic planning process. Use The Gartner Group as one source of very credible opinions.

As you assess your overall corporate technology needs, you'll also need to take a hard look at your client software and Web site innovation. These are two very fast moving areas of the Internet.

Don't forget that basic server infrastructure technology evolves at a fairly slow pace, but the technology that touches end-users evolves at a very rapid pace. When the competition is hot and the technology is changing rapidly, you'll typically see major upgrades and changes every six months.

Just to put this in a historical framework, recall from an earlier discussion in this Appendix that, when browsers first came out in about 1995, there was about a $3-billion market for terminal emulators and TCP/IP packages. A number of companies were producing the software that would sit on your PC and run TCP/IP. This gave people access to the basic networking services like file transfer (ftp) and Telnet, which was the terminal emulation software that people were using at the time. Telnet allowed you to replace a set of dedicated terminals with a much less expensive solution.

A number of firms were in the $1-billion range with Telnet software at the time, but that software got wiped out in a period of about two years when it was replaced by the Web browser. Therefore, the whole Telnet market basically vaporized because it was replaced by the Web interface, which became, almost overnight, the dominant way to interface back into legacy systems.

The key point to remember is that client software can change very rapidly. During the early days of the browser wars when Microsoft and Netscape were going at each other, they were releasing new updates to the browser every six months or so. At that point, these updates were seriously meaty. We've now gotten to the point where things are pretty static, and we're not seeing very rapid updates anymore. Most updates are happening in the area of security.

Consider the changing nature of Web sites. These can be updated minute by minute if you want. This is the area where you will find the most rapidly occurring changes. The strength of the Web is that you can change your Web site on the fly, and everyone can see your changes instantaneously.

The best companies understand that they need to tweak their Web sites constantly. However, it's important to recognize that different companies have different timelines, cycles, and needs for updating their sites. Make sure you're not overinvesting in upgrades that you really don't need and underinvesting in areas in which innovation can really make an important business contribution. If you upgrade too often, your customers become frustrated because they can't find what they want. It's kind of like rearranging the items in the grocery store too often. If you don't upgrade often enough, your customers don't find timely and relevant information, and you lose them again.

Frankly, I find too many companies leave their Web sites too static for too long. These companies tend to overinvest in the backend. I think you're better off investing a bit more in the frontend where you interact with customers.

Nevertheless, you should still reengineer your backend every two to three years. If you don't do this, your backend won't be capable of evolving quickly enough to keep up with your frontend. Look at it this way. Your user interface is kind of a small wheel, and it's spinning around very fast. Your server is the bigger gear. It moves around slowly, but, if it doesn't keep moving, the whole process gets jammed. Think of your network infrastructure as one of those large gears and keep updating it every two to three years.

With regard to **application deployment**, you may have noticed that your server infrastructure has become unwieldy and complex because you have a lot of special purpose servers doing special functions. You can easily end up with servers on the other side of the world with cross-linked functionality through the URL. However, the network between these two servers can be very expensive and very unreliable. Unless you take the time to examine your site architecture on a regular basis, you can end up with major performance problems, some of which happen at mission-critical times.

To avoid these pitfalls, it's important to use a number of great tools on the market that can help you analyze all of your linkages, analyze how people are using your site, and analyze your delivery architecture. You'll need people who are experts in delivery architecture to help you with this. These are specialists whose skill sets transcend applications development.

Again, I must alert you to the sad reality that less than 2 or 3 percent of the people who present themselves as Web developers actually have an advanced degree of competence. Therefore choose your experts carefully.

Here's some welcome good news, however. The entry barriers to putting information up on the Web are very low. You can buy a book on HTML, and, if you can use a word processor, you can create your own HTML code. In no time flat, you can put up your own Web site. If you do it yourself, it may not look glamorous, but it still could be quite functional.

When you're ready to scale up your site and turn it into a high-performance function, search for those developers possessing the rare talent for making a Web site rock solid.

You'll also want to consider some of the third parties out there that might be able to do some testing and assessment of your Web site. Some of the better hosting vendors also can offer excellent assistance in this area. They can also help you understand where your risk factors and scalability factors are. This information can be an important factor in operating your site profitably.

Be sure to take the time to understand what kind of traffic you can expect to see on your site, along with other information such as your overall site maintenance costs and operating expenses. I've found that a lot of Web-hosting companies bid low and don't take any time to look at your infrastructure. This has often caused their clients to lose money. The sad fact is that, with just a few changes in the applications, huge improvements can be realized.

A good hosting company quite often will have a preferred architecture for deployment. This can be particularly helpful when you need to scale your site rapidly. A good hosting company can wheel hardware in so you can access greater capacity more quickly. If you have a failure, a good hosting company can wheel hardware in to have you up and running again quickly.

You've now come to the end of your first postgraduate technology course.

To sum it all up, I'm not proposing that business executives need to become technology specialists. However, a little bit of time spent just thinking through the strategic possibilities of technology will give you a better sense of the rate and pace of development that you should pursue. It also will help prevent you from going off the edge of the cliff on a technology fad.

Here is one final thought. Please keep in mind that it's equally dangerous to stay on the cliff when the cliff is about to collapse. In other words, if the world has moved on and you're still standing there, you might be standing on a structure that is about to collapse. However, if you're tuned in to the latest Internet technology, you're about to embark on the fast track to profit.

Bibliography

Online Sources

1. ABN-AMRO (http://www.abnamro.com)
2. Amazon.com (http://www.amazon.com)
3. American Poems (http://www.americanpoems.com)
4. American Society of Travel Agents (http://www.astanet.com)
5. AT&T (http://www.att.com)
6. BIPS Worldwide (http://www.bips-worldwide.com)
7. Business Innovation & Technology Services (http://bits.corp.hp.com)
8. Celebrate Today (http://www.celebratetoday.com)
9. Christie's (http://www.christies.com)
10. Chrysler (http://www.chrysler.com)
11. CommWeb (http://www.comweb.com)
12. eSATCOM.net (http://www.esatcom.net)
13. European Union (http://europa.eu.int/ISPO/telecompolicy/en/Study-en.htm)
14. Federal Deposit Insurance Corporation (http://www.fdic.gov)
15. Fidelity (http://www.fidelity.com)
16. Financial Service Facts (http://www.financialservicefacts.org)
17. Ford Motor Company (http://www.fordmotorcompany.com)
18. General Motors Corporation (http://www.gm.com)
19. Glamournet.com (http://glamournet.com)
20. Internet Society (http://www.isoc.org)
21. International Telecommunications Union (http://www.itu.int)

22. Inventors (http://inventors.about.com)
23. Page Six.com (http://www.pagesix.com)
24. Public Broadcasting Service (http://www.pbs.org)
25. Sabre (http://www.sabre.com)
26. SITA (http://www.sita.com)
27. Snopes (http://www.snopes2.com)
28. Sothebys.com (http://www.sothebys.com)
29. Telecommunications Industry Association (http://www.tiaonline.org)
30. TelecomWriting.com (http://www.privateline.com)
31. United Airlines (http://www.ual.com)
32. Useless Knowledge.com (http://www.uselessknowledge.com)
33. U.S. Federal Communications Commission (http://www.fcc.gov)
34. U.S. National Telecommunications and Information Administration (http://www.ntia.doc.gov)
35. USSA (http://www.usaa.com)

Index

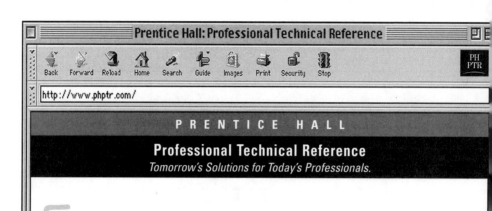